MW00786270

The Language of Fear

Piotr Cap

The Language
of Fear

Communicating Threat in Public Discourse

Piotr Cap
Department of Pragmatics
University of Łódź
Łódź, Poland

ISBN 978-1-137-59729-8   ISBN 978-1-137-59731-1 (eBook)
DOI 10.1057/978-1-137-59731-1

Library of Congress Control Number: 2016952434

Cover illustration: Pattern adapted from an Indian cotton print produced in the 19th century

Printed on acid-free paper

This Palgrave Macmillan imprint is published by Springer Nature
The registered company is Macmillan Publishers Ltd.
The registered company address is: The Campus, 4 Crinan Street, London, N1 9XW, United Kingdom

CONTENTS

LIST OF FIGURES

LIST OF TABLES

INTRODUCTION

This book has two aims: empirical and theoretical. The empirical aim is to study patterns of threat construction and fear generation in contemporary public communication, including state political discourse as well as non-governmental, media and institutional discourse on issues of public concern, such as health, environment and technology. We argue that most public communication is inherently coercive, involving a variety of discursive strategies by which the top actors (political, organizational and business leaders) legitimize their goals, actions and policies. We claim that manufacturing fear and social anxiety is a central feature of modern public discourse, serving to justify policies which include the policy-makers and their audiences in a joint course of action aimed to prevent or neutralize the threat. The book documents these claims in examples from a number of American as well as European discourses, including presidential speeches, journalistic opinions and organizational reports. The approach is essentially critical discourse analytic, combining insights from pragmatics, cognitive linguistics, text linguistics and several non-linguistic theories within social and political sciences. In particular, the book employs the apparatus of Proximization Theory (PT). PT is a recent model of crisis construction and threat generation which has been developed to account for the ways in which the discursive construction of closeness and remoteness can be manipulated in the public sphere and bound up with fear, security and conflict. Originally designed to deal with instances of state political communication (presidential addresses, parliamentary debates), PT is used in the book to cover an extended spectrum of public discourses, from immigration debates to anti-tobacco campaigns.

Proving the suitability of PT to explore such a broad and eclectic collection of discourses constitutes the second, theoretical aim of the book.

The book comprises 6 chapters, followed by a brief Conclusion. Chapter 1 contains a discussion on the nature of fear and threat and how they affect public audiences, as well as motivate them to act. It introduces the relevant theoretical concepts, such as coercion, legitimization and delegitimization. Chapter 2 describes the main tenets of PT and its applicability to work with the above concepts to account for acts of coercion in 'state political' and, potentially, 'public' discourse. Chapters 3–6 are case studies in which PT is used to analyse four different public discourses: health, environment, technology and immigration. The Conclusion reflects on the fear and threat generation patterns in these discourses and how successful PT has been in elucidating them.

CHAPTER 1

Cognitive, Social and Psychological Issues of Public Discourse and Threat Communication

Abstract This opening chapter contains an interdisciplinary discussion on the nature of threat and fear and how they affect the audience in public discourse. It introduces relevant theoretical concepts, such as coercion, legitimization and delegitimization. It demonstrates that threatening visions and anticipations appeal to the public as long as they are considered personally consequential. This socio-psychological premise is taken as a prerequisite for the development of Proximization Theory.

Keywords Threat communication · Coercion · Legitimization · Delegitimization · Credibility

What is public discourse? Depending on the discipline one is constructing a definition from what this term constitutes may differ. In this book, the term 'public discourse' is used to refer to communicated issues of public culture and public concern that affect individuals and groups in a given civilization. Public discourse is understood, after Jürgen Habermas (1981), as a collection of voices on top issues of politics, economy, law, education, and other areas of public interest and participation. Since in a nation-state some of these voices are naturally more powerful than others, a bulk of public discourse is produced – or at least initiated – by political leaders, as well as institutional bodies regulating social practices

© The Author(s) 2017   1
P. Cap, *The Language of Fear*, DOI 10.1057/978-1-137-59731-1_1

in different domains of life. It is this large and dominant part of public discourse that the present book focuses on.

Public discourse is essentially strategic: there exist observable and systematic ways in which interests of the top actors – politicians, institutional leaders, lawmakers, media management – are performed linguistically. Public leaders use a plethora of rhetorical means to manage their power, status and credibility in the service of a social consensus. The aim is to receive people's approval of policies involving both sides, the leader and her audience, in a joint course of action. In the words of Habermas (1981), public communication – including state political discourse as well as voices of various non-governmental bodies and 'grass-roots' initiatives – has the continual goal of maximizing the number of 'shared visions', that is, common conceptions of current reality as well as its desired developments.

COERCION, LEGITIMIZATION AND DELEGITIMIZATION

As such, public communication emerges as necessarily coercive. Public actors behave coercively in a variety of ways – setting agendas, selecting topics in conversation, positioning the self and others in specific relationships, making assumptions about realities that their hearers are obliged to at least temporarily accept in order to process the text or talk. Power can also be exercised through the control of others' use of language – that is, through various kinds and degrees of censorship and access control. The latter include the structure and management of the media, the arena where much public communication takes place (Fetzer and Lauerbach 2007). Another important language-related phenomenon that could be judged coercive is the strategic stimulation of affect. Although the precise details are still under-researched, it is reasonable to hypothesize links between meaning structures produced via discourse (Chilton 2004, 2014). Putting it simply, certain kinds of texts can stimulate certain hormones, and the effect may be automatic.

Coercion strategies almost always involve legitimization, except in the extreme case, where it is questionable that one is still in the realm of what is understood by 'politics', 'public sphere' and the like. Legitimization is a complex concept and a complex practice involving, first of all, a linguistic enactment of the speaker's right to be obeyed (Chilton 2004; Cap 2008). The claim to rightness and the resulting enactment of legitimization mean that the speaker's rhetoric is grounded in her implicit claim to inhabit a particular social role, and to possess a particular authority (Martin and Wodak 2003). The possession of authority provides argumentative rationale for listing reasons to be obeyed (Van Eemeren and Grootendorst 2004). This involves a symbolic assignment of different ideological values to different discourse parties, the assertion of hearers' wants in the moment of crisis and, crucially, the construal of charismatic leadership needed to handle the crisis situation (Huntington 2004). All these practices are components of successful legitimization, whose central objective is a broad social mobilization around a common goal. Legitimization can thus be 'a good means to a good end', as well as 'a bad means to a bad end' (Hartman 2002). A telling example of the former is legitimization of the 'war on cancer', which we discuss in Chap. 3.

The essential counterpart of legitimization is delegitimization (Chilton 2004; Cap 2006, 2008): others (foreigners, 'enemies within', political opposition, institutional adversaries, etc.) are presented negatively, and the techniques include the use of ideas of difference and (geographical, cultural) boundaries. The strategies of delegitimization (of the Other) and legitimization (of the Self) may thus be conceptualized as lying at opposite ends of a scale. Delegitimization can manifest itself in acts of negative other-presentation, acts of blaming, scape-goating, marginalizing, excluding, attacking the moral character of some individual or group, attacking the rationality and sanity of the other. The extreme is to deny the humanness of the other. This can be seen in several interventionist discourses of today, for instance the Western narrative against the Islamic State (ISIS). At the other end of the spectrum legitimization, usually oriented to the Self, includes positive self-presentation, manifesting itself in acts of self-praise, self-apology, self-explanation, self-justification, self-identification as a source of authority, reason, vision and sanity, where the self is either an individual (political or institutional leader) or the group with which the individual identifies or wishes to identify.

FROM 'SELF AND OTHER' TO THREAT AND FEAR

The Self–Other distinction and the related coercion, legitimization and delegitimization strategies are a stable property of public discourse, deriving their strength from anthropological developments. In his classic discussion of the co-evolution of language and the public sphere, Hockett (1960) notes the two-tier organization of human socio-political awareness and behaviour. On the one hand, people possess a mental ability to structure their cognitive experience ('looking at' the world) in terms of dichotomous representations of good and evil, right and wrong, acceptable and unacceptable, etc. On the other hand, they possess a strictly linguistic ability to evoke or reinforce these dichotomous representations in accordance with their social goals. The central goal involves, let us repeat, getting others to share a common view on what is good/evil, right/wrong, acceptable/unacceptable, etc., and consequently, on how to secure the 'right', 'good', 'useful', 'acceptable', 'just', against a possible intrusion, in the life of a society, of the 'wrong', 'evil', 'harmful', etc. Thus, public communication nearly always presupposes *distance* between the Self party (the home group and its leaders) and the Other party (the possible 'intruder'). The more specific the Self party and the more consequential or broader the goals (as in state political discourse), the clearer the marking of the distance through linguistic means. The 'good' and 'right' are thus conceptualized and then lexicalized as 'close to Self' and the 'wrong' and 'evil' as 'remote to Self'.

Discourse Representations

Several models have been proposed to account for this cognitive–linguistic interplay, such as 'text worlds' (Fauconnier 1985; Werth 1999; Gavins 2007) and 'discourse spaces' (Levinson 2003; Chilton 2004, 2014). Text World Theory (Gavins 2007), Deictic Space Theory (Chilton 2004, 2014) and the theory of spatio-temporal frames of reference (Levinson 2003) all agree that texts/discourses enable hearers to generate cognitive structures in short- and long-term memory, as it were backstage rather than upfront in the words themselves. We can think of such structures – 'spaces' or 'worlds' – as *discourse ontologies.* All forms of public communication make assumptions about what there *is* in the public sphere – what social entities exist and what are the relationships between them, including physical distance as well as, usually, ideological/moral distance. The basic architecture of a discourse space (DS) is thus as follows (Fig. 1.1):

While this core bipolar arrangement of the DS is seldom disputed, controversies arise with regard to the many and different ways in which the distance between the Self and the Other can be defined. There is first of all – as has been noted – physical or spatial distance, but the other dimensions are far less obvious. In his influential Deictic Space Theory (DST), Chilton (2004, 2014) acknowledges the primacy of the spatial dimension and recognizes two accompanying dimensions, temporal and

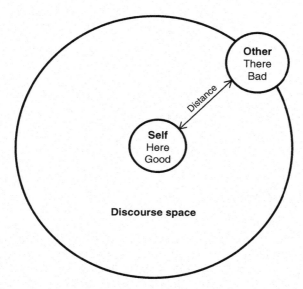

Fig. 1.1 Discourse space (DS)

modal, both of which involve conceptualizations in spatial terms. Time is conceptualized in terms of motion through space ('the time to act has arrived') and modality is conceptualized in terms of distance ('remotely possible') or (deontic modality) as a metaphoric extension of a binary opposition between the close and the remote. The origin of the three dimensions is at the *deictic centre*, which includes the symbolically marked Self, that is *I, we*, etc. All other entities and processes exist relative to ontological spaces defined by their coordinates on the space (s), time (t) and modality (m) axes. We may call these spaces 'dimensions of deixis' (Fig. 1.2), which allow communicators to process the ongoing kaleidoscope of ontological configurations activated by text.

Figure 1.2 can be taken as a three-dimensional elaboration on the distance relation shown in Fig. 1.1. Assuming that distance is crucial to the account of the Self–Other dichotomy, it offers a useful pre-requisite for studying different linguistic ways of 'othering'; that is the many ways in which top public actors depict their socio-political adversaries as a distant yet real threat to the group (or nation, in state political discourse) that they represent and speak for. By way of illustration, let us use the 'bare' geometrical arrangement in

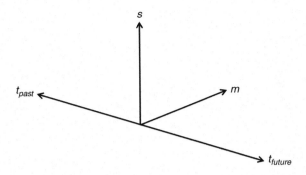

Fig. 1.2   Dimensions of deixis

Fig. 1.1 to create a full-fledged three-dimensional representation of one of the presidential addresses analysed in Chilton (2004). The excerpt below comes from a speech by President Bill Clinton, in which he prepares Americans for the US intervention in Kosovo on 24 March 1999[1]:

(25) Ending this tragedy is a moral imperative. (26) It is also important to America's national interest. (27) Take a look at this map. (28) Kosovo is a small place, but it sits on a major fault line between Europe, Asia and the Middle East, at the meeting place of Islam and both the Western and Orthodox branches of Christianity. (29) To the south are our allies, Greece and Turkey; to the north, our new democratic allies in Central Europe. (30) And all around Kosovo there are other small countries, struggling with their own economic and political challenges – countries that could be overwhelmed by a large, new wave of refugees from Kosovo. (31) All the ingredients for a major war are there: ancient grievances, struggling democracies, and in the center of it all a dictator in Serbia who has done nothing since the Cold War ended but start new wars and pour gasoline on the flames of ethnic and religious division. (32) Sarajevo, the capital of neighboring Bosnia, is where World War I began. (33) World War II and the Holocaust engulfed this region. (34) In both wars Europe was slow to recognize the dangers, and the United States waited even longer to enter the conflicts. (35) Just imagine if leaders back then had acted wisely and early enough, how many lives could have been saved, how many Americans would not have had to die. (36) We learned some of the same lessons in Bosnia just a few years ago. (37) The world did not act early enough to stop that war, either.

The emerging conceptual-lexical representation (Fig. 1.3 below; the numbers refer to sentences or [30'–31'] parts of sentences responsible for a particular conceptual operation) can be described as follows. At the intersection point (the origin) of the three axes is 'this map' (President Clinton is seen pointing to a visual aid). The map itself does not represent an objective reality; its task is to launch a reality space to be specified by the verbal commentary. A presupposition obtains: addressees must, in order to interpret the unfolding text as coherent, infer that (27) and the following sentences are intended to motivate (26) (that national interests are at stake) and (25) (that action is a moral imperative). On that premise, sentences (28), (29) and (30) serve to set up a 'map representation' space. This construal involves a conventional pragmatic function, by which cartographic images are taken to represent objective reality spaces (Fauconnier and

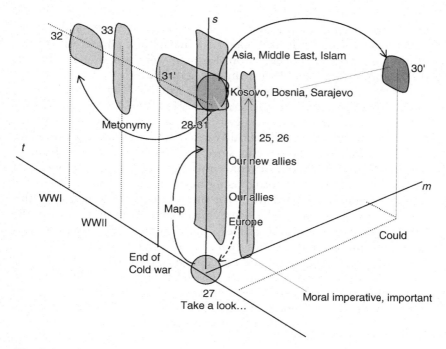

Fig. 1.3 Events located on spatial, temporal and modal axes

Turner 2002). 'This map' in the studio (or 'in' the viewer's area) represents a conceptual space that is mutually understood as remote ('there' in [31]), but which the map presented 'here' and 'now' makes conceptually close. In the process of defining the map's conceptual projection space the use of 'could' ([30']) in 'countries that could be overwhelmed by a large new wave of refugees from Kosovo') prompts the addressee to launch a space at the possibility point of m and in the near future zone of t. This is *not* part of the televised map picture; it is part of the conceptual 'picture' produced by the discourse, which conflates the apparently remote Kosovo space and addressee space. The resulting proximity of the Kosovo space and its negatively charged Other-entities (as opposed to the positively charged Self-entities [President Clinton, his audience, allies in Europe] in the deictic centre) allows transition to (31), which expresses a generalized likelihood of a major military conflict and thus threat to American interests. In (31), the positioning of the (31') embedded clause ('...who has done nothing since the Cold War but start new wars and pour gasoline on the flames of ethnic and religious divisions') as a syntactic and intonational focus furthers this likelihood by a metaphoric phrase: the 'flames of divisions' (refugees fleeing from Kosovo) will cause a major 'fire' in the region as they 'meet' with (more) 'gasoline'.

On the t axis, the geopolitical space is extended 'backwards', metonymically, by reference to the spatial location 'Sarajevo' (32). Kosovo is linked to Sarajevo, and Sarajevo is linked metonymically to World War I, and World War I to World War II and the Holocaust. The links can be considered metonymic since the relation between Kosovo, Sarajevo and WWI is one of conceptual 'contiguity' in a geopolitical frame which holds events progressing from the remote past toward the present. 'Sarajevo' is used to evoke the whole WWI frame, and 'this region' (33) is used in the same metonymic fashion to evoke the WWII and the Holocaust frames. These discursively linked frames constitute the groundwork for two sets of generalizations: (31) relating to the geographical space conceptualized 'around' Kosovo, and (34)–(35) relating to a flashback historical space conceptualized in connection with Sarajevo. These generalizations are used in turn to wrap up the entire representation ([36]–[37]) and justify its initial point (25), that is a moral imperative to act.

Threats at the Doorstep

The strength of models such as Chilton's DST lies in showing how discourse can be used to express the Self–Other opposition in terms of a clear and potentially growing threat – such as the threat to US allies in Europe following the possible escalation of the Kosovo war. The discourse of threat has a coercive function: it generates fear and as a result facilitates strong leadership. It also possesses a legitimizing function, in that it offers a quick and easy rationale for following an actor who claims the ability and thus the right to handle the crisis situation.

In public communication, the effectiveness of threat relies much on the conceptualization of personal consequences it involves (Bandura 1986; Zimbardo and Leippe 1991). Public audiences are normally reluctant to accept and legitimate radical policies unless they are proposed as a response to developments posing direct danger to particular groups or individuals. The danger may be construed as physical and involving an emerging threat to life, as in the Kosovo example or other discourses of military intervention. On many occasions, however, the endangered elements are the quality of life, the functioning of a given social structure as well as individual interests of people. Thus, the construal of imminent danger paves the way for legitimization of preventive measures in a vast number of public discourses. These include public health, environment, technology, migration, education and many other domains.

The enforcement of imminent personal threat often involves *analogy*, which sets up a link between the current crisis situation and a past situation in which the threat materialized as a result of negligence. Silberstein (2004) observes that much of the contemporary anti-terrorist rhetoric, especially the rhetoric after the 9/11 attacks, includes strong claims of 'inaction' following the UN anti-terrorist diplomatic resolutions of the 1990s. This fact has been often used as a 'lesson from the past' and 'for the future', legitimizing prompt response and military measures. Similar voices could be heard after the Paris 2015 attacks instigated by the ISIS. In his 14 November 2015 address to the nation, President Francois Hollande announced a French air operation on the city of Raqqa in an attempt to destroy the ISIS headquarters in Syria. At the same time, he called the earlier coalition-led efforts 'inadequate' and in fact making the ISIS threat grow.

CREDIBILITY

The construction of analogy, as well as other carriers of fear-based legit-imization, relies for success on the credibility of the speaker. This includes enactment of credibility for a new legitimization case, maintaining cred-ibility notwithstanding contextual developments which undermine it, and, notably, re-enactment of credibility after it has been temporarily damaged/lost. There are two classic theories which are relevant for each of these three situations. The *latitude of acceptance theory* (Sherif and Hovland 1961; Kiesler et al. 1969; Jowett and O'Donnell 1992) main-tains that the best credibility (and thus legitimization) effects can be expected if public speaker produces her message in line with the psycho-logical, social, political, cultural, religious, etc., predispositions of the addressee (Jowett and O'Donnell 1992). However, since full compliance is almost never possible, it is essential that the novel message is at least tentatively or partly acceptable – then, its acceptability and the speaker's credibility are going to increase with time. This is where *consistency theory* starts. Festinger (1957) observes that the increase in credibility over time can be attributed to human drive toward *consistency in belief.* Namely, people possess the need for 'homeostasis', a state of mental stability. This means that, in the long run, they do not tolerate dissonance in their judgements, especially with regard to the same or similar issues. Consequently, whenever faced with a new message producing a potential conflict with the existing ideological, psychological or moral groundwork, people go to great lengths trying to see any positive aspects of the message so it could be internalized as an element of the groundwork. Naturally, the precondition obtains that the message is not entirely reject-able from the very beginning; at least some parts of it must be congruent with the addressee's predispositions.

Issues of credibility in public discourse have also been investigated by cognitive-evolutionary theories, such as *cheater detection module* (Axelrod 1984; Cosmides 1989; Sperber 2000; etc.). The cheater detection module has been originally (Axelrod 1984; Cosmides 1989) considered a logico-rhetorical device that evolved in human cognition to resist acts of deception, through the checking of speaker's coherence. This basic char-acterization has undergone several modifications, which involve seeing the module not only as addressee's defense mechanism but also as speaker's persuasion tool, particularly useful in threat communication. In Dan Sperber's (2000, p. 136) words, for addressees the module is 'a means to filter communicated information', but for speakers it is 'a means to penetrate the filters of others'. In this communicative 'arms race', public speakers make strategic displays of discourse coherence to neutralize the operation of the cheater detection module in the addressee so as to force their legitimization strategies.

The linguistic approaches to credibility provide a useful elaboration on specific structures and discourse forms responsible for actual legitimization and coercion acts. Within linguistic pragmatics, credibility issues have been investigated in terms of the illocutionary force and perlocutionary effects of speech acts, most commonly the act of *assertion*. Assertions are helpful in establishing speaker's credibility due to several content features and pragmalinguistic functions, including predication of facts, reference to undeniable and/or historically accepted (ideological) groundworks, enactment of ideological 'common ground' uniting the speaker and the addressee, expression of beliefs (often implying actions) being currently in line with the addressee's predispositions (Jary 2010). Assertions seldom perform their job individually; they tend to appear in sequences which collectively build up the credibility needed to pursue actions or policies. Assertions are thus instrumental in setting up an 'assertion-directive link' (Cap 2002), which involves sanctioning controversial future acts based on trust the speaker has earned in her (thus far) uncontroversial rhetoric.

Another pragmatic concept bound up with credibility is *implicature* (Grice 1975; Levinson 2000; Horn 2004), which plays a key role in maintaining legitimization over time. Implicature has the power to launch a vast spectrum of possible meanings interpreted differently by different addressees in accordance with their different pre-expectations, wants and needs. Since any such inferences can be 'cancelled' in prospective discourse (i.e. by adding more content), implicature not only helps legitimization in current reality, but also in the future, 'updated' reality, where it redefines and re-legitimizes actions for the new context and new predispositions or priorities of the addressee. The process where public speaker monitors the current needs of the addressee, enforcing or cancelling inferences accordingly, reflects operation of the cheater detection module: the speaker is constantly sensitive to whether her original message or legitimization pattern are still coherent and still work for the addressee or there is already a need to alter the rhetoric. An example of such a turning point is the transition that occurred in the US interventionist discourse when, around November 2003, the world learned there were no WMD (weapons of mass destruction) in Iraq (Cap 2013). This meant that the Bush administration had to find a new legitimization premise for the Iraq war, yet without making nonsense of the original premise of 'direct threat'. Consequently, the phrase 'programs for WMD' was coined at the end of 2003, replacing the initial 'WMD'. The function of the new phrase was to induce two apparently disparate inferences at the same time: one seeing WMD as a 'product' in accordance with the original premise, and the other seeing it as a vague 'conception'.

Credibility and legitimization issues have also been addressed by text and corpus linguistics, especially in the area of internal and external coherence of texts (Hart 2010, pp. 92–94), offering a much needed linguistic addition to cognitive models such as cheater detection. As far as internal coherence is concerned, Gough and Talbot (1996) indicate that legitimization of assertions is greatly enhanced by the use of *logical terms* ('and', 'or', 'if') and items marking *inferential relationships* ('therefore', 'since', 'nevertheless', etc.). These terms are considered adaptive devices for persuasion, facilitating acceptance of ideational information and 'cueing ideological assumptions' (Fairclough 1989, p. 109). Regarding external coherence, scholars have stressed the role of *evidentiality* (the linguistic marking of evidence) as a source of reliability of assertions. For example, Bednarek (2006) identifies four specified bases of knowledge used as evidence in the British newspaper reporting of transnational crises: (i) Perception; (ii) General Knowledge; (iii) Proof; (iv) Obviousness. These bases of knowledge legitimize assertions in different ways, drawing on different types of evidence. *Perception* provides directly attested sensory evidence, whose existence is indicated in discourse by phrases such as 'it appears that' or 'visibly'. The evidence is construed as acquired directly via visual perception or as something made available to see. Evidence from *General Knowledge* is 'marked as based on what is regarded as part of the communal epistemic background' (Bednarek 2006, p. 640) and the most typical markers are 'widely held [view(s), opinion(s)]' and 'everybody knows (it/that)'. Hart (2010) observes that this pattern of legitimization reflects what Van Leeuwen and Wodak (1999) call 'conformity authorization', involving the *ad populum* fallacy that something is true if everyone believes it. *Proof* is expressed by markers such as 'research', 'results', 'statistics', etc., which 'show', 'indicate' or 'reveal' facts; as such, *Proof* often overlaps with *Perception*. Finally, *Obviousness* provides evidence from so-called facts of life – self-evident claims containing phrases such as 'obviously' or 'clearly'.

Lastly, applied studies point out that legitimization of assertions, especially those expressing strong and imminent threats, benefits a lot from *source-tagging*, a judgement attribution strategy whereby an antecedent authorial voice is invoked ('...experts warned that...'; '...specialist think tank established that...') to communicate sensitive or potentially controversial information (Groom 2000; Hunston 2000). The credibility of the assertion rises as a result, as does the credibility of any subsequent discourse drawing upon the initial legitimization effect. Source-tagging is thus a macro-functional strategy, particularly useful in long-term legitimization.

Findings Thus Far

We have discussed in this chapter the most important concepts associated with public discourse and power relations in public communication, such as enactment of leadership, coercion, legitimization and credibility. These concepts define phenomena which underlie and characterize public discourse as a strategic, goal-oriented undertaking in which the top actors aim at a broad public acceptance of policies benefitting the social or political group that they represent. To accomplish this aim, public leaders tend to legitimize their actions or proposals for action in terms of oppositions between right and wrong, good and evil, acceptable and unacceptable. As a result, most public communication operates indexically, with a view to enacting social and political affiliations and distinctions. These distinctions are embedded in mental representations that public leaders continually define, enforce, negotiate and redefine through language, to maximize the number of shared visions of reality.

The default representation that serves as an anchor for all further conceptualizations is the Self vs. Other opposition, which involves physical as well as ideological distance between the home party (the leader's social group) and the foreign party (the group or entity which the leader defines as adversarial). The presence of the adversarial group or entity is construed as a threat to interests of the home group. The construction of threat is aimed at generating public fear, which in turn helps legitimization of (preventive) policies. Legitimization effects are likely to be the greatest if, first, the threat is presented as imminent and global yet personally consequential; second, it is communicated by a credible speaker who observes predispositions of her addressee.

The analysis of threat communication in public discourse is best carried out within models which recognize the Self–Other arrangement and thus the dichotomous character of the DS. We have found such a potential in several cognitive-linguistic theories, particularly the Deictic Space Theory proposed by Chilton (2004, 2014). Indeed, DST can be successfully used to express the Self vs. Other opposition in terms of a clear and potentially growing threat. It properly recognizes that the threat has a coercive function of generating fear and as a result facilitating strong leadership on the public arena. However, Chilton's DST has rather little to say about how the threat is actually *performed*. That is, while it shows what typical lexico-grammatical choices are available to define the remote Other as a static entity, it does not account for the discursive ways to make it dynamic and encroach on the Self entity – the speaker's home group. For this, we need a related but essentially different theory, which we describe in the next chapter.

NOTE

1. Numbering original (Chilton 2004, p. 142).

CHAPTER 2

Proximization: A Threat-Based Model of Policy Legitimization

Abstract This chapter outlines the main tenets of Proximization Theory (PT). It defines proximization as a discursive strategy of presenting the apparently remote events and ideologies as increasingly consequential to the speaker and her addressee. Working with examples from the discourse of the War on Terror, it reveals how threatening visions are invoked to obtain legitimization of preventive actions and policies. The chapter proposes that the success of PT in describing legitimization patterns in state political discourse warrants its extended application to other discourses in the public domain.

Keywords Legitimization · Proximization · Proximization Theory · Self and Other · State political discourse

We have seen in the opening chapter how discourse can be used to structure socio-political realities in terms of conceptual oppositions between the home group (Self) and the apparently remote out-group (Other). The Self–Other dichotomy constitutes a basis for construing the presence of the out-group as a growing threat and thus a premise for response from the home group. We have discussed discourse models, particularly Deictic Space Theory (DST), which account for this dichotomy and how it underlies the fear-based rhetoric of legitimization.

© The Author(s) 2017
P. Cap, *The Language of Fear*, DOI 10.1057/978-1-137-59731-1_2

It should be evident by now that the focus of DST is on the basic or default arrangement of the discourse space (DS), where Self and Other are located at a set distance from each other. This means that DST is ideally suited to analyse discourse representations of the fixed positioning of the two groups of entities and the ominous *presence* of the Other as the source of all threat. At the same time, however, it is not very well suited to account for the important mechanism of the realization, or performance, of the threat. That is, it does not provide tools, including lexical and grammatical patterns, to study the discursive construal of *movement* of the Other as the central threat element. In this chapter we introduce a model that integrates the DST perspective with a cognitive-pragmatic perspective on discourse as the vehicle of such a movement and DS re-arrangement.

PROXIMIZATION AND PROXIMIZATION THEORY

In its broadest sense, proximization is a discursive strategy of presenting physically and temporally distant events or states of affairs (including 'distant', i.e. adversarial ideologies) as increasingly and negatively consequential to the speaker and her addressee. Projecting distant entities as gradually encroaching upon the speaker–addressee territory (both physical and ideological), the speaker seeks legitimization of actions and policies she proposes to neutralize the growing impact of the negative, 'foreign', 'alien', 'antagonistic', entities.

The term 'proximization' was first proposed by Cap to analyse coercion patterns in the US anti-terrorist rhetoric following 9/11 (Cap 2006, 2008, 2010). Since then it has been used within different discourse domains, though most commonly in studies of *state political discourses*: crisis construction and war rhetoric (Chovanec 2010), anti-migration discourse (e.g. Hart 2010), political party representation (Cienki et al. 2010), construction of national memory and design of foreign policy documents (Dunmire 2011). Findings from these studies have been integrated in the Proximization Theory (PT) put forward in Cap (2013). PT follows the original concept of proximization, which is defined as a forced construal operation meant to evoke closeness of the external threat, to solicit legitimization of preventive measures. The threat comes from DS-peripheral entities, referred to as outside-deictic-centre (ODCs) entities, which are conceptualized to be crossing the Space to invade the inside-deictic-centre (IDC) entities, the speaker and her addressee. The threat possesses a spatio-temporal as well as ideological nature, which means that proximization can be considered in three aspects. 'Spatial proximization' is a forced construal of the DS peripheral entities encroaching *physically* upon the DS central entities (speaker, addressee). Analogously to Chilton's DST, the spatial aspect of proximization is primary as the remaining aspects or strategies involve conceptualizations in spatial terms. 'Temporal proximization' is a forced construal of the envisaged conflict as not only imminent, but also momentous, historic and thus needing immediate response and unique preventive measures. Spatial and temporal proximization involve fear appeals (becoming particularly strong in reactionary political projects) and typically use analogies to conflate the growing threat with an actual disastrous occurrence in the past, to endorse the current scenario. Lastly, 'axiological proximization' involves construal of a gathering ideological clash between the 'home values' of the DS central entities (IDCs) and the alien, antagonistic (ODC) values. Importantly, the ODC values are construed to reveal potential to materialize (i.e., prompt a physical impact) within the IDC, the speaker's and the addressee's, home territory.

Altogether, PT subsumes a dynamic conception of the DS, which involves not only the opposition between IDC entities (i.e. Self entities, as defined by earlier DS models) and ODC (i.e. Other) entities, but also the discursively constructed movement of the latter towards the centre of the DS (Fig. 2.1 – compare Fig. 1.1). It thus focuses, from a linguistic standpoint, on the *lexical and grammatical deictic choices* speakers make to, first, index the existing socio-political and ideological distinctions and, second, demonstrate the capacity of the out-group to erase these distinctions by forcibly colonizing the in-group's space.

PT holds that all the three strategies of proximization contribute to the *continual narrowing of the symbolic distance* between the entities or values in DS and their negative impact on the speaker and her addressee. This does not mean, however, that all the three strategies are linguistically present (to the same degree) throughout each stretch of the unfolding discourse. While any use of proximization principally subsumes all of its strategies, spatial, temporal and axiological, the degree of their actual representation in text is continually motivated by their effectiveness in the evolving context. Extralinguistic contextual developments may cause the speaker to limit the use of one strategy and compensate it by an increased use of another, in the interest of the continuity of legitimization.

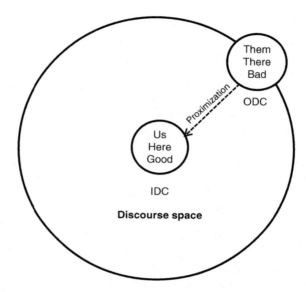

Fig. 2.1   Proximization in discourse space (DS)

Compared to discourse representations discussed in Chap. 1, PT makes a new contribution at two levels, (i) cognitive-pragmatic and (ii) linguistic, or more precisely, lexico-grammatical. At the (i) cognitive-pragmatic conceptual level, the Spatial-Temporal-Axiological (STA) model of proximization revisits the ontological status and pragmatic function of deixis and deictic markers. Deixis has been traditionally considered (Levinson 1983; Levelt 1989) a merely technical necessity for the possible interpretability of communication. On the proximization approach deixis constitutes more than a formal tool for the coding of elements of context to make all communication possible. It is potentially an instrument (or a component thereof) for legitimization, persuasion and social coercion. Within PT, the concept of deixis is not *reduced* to a finite set of 'deictic expressions', but rather *expanded* to include bigger lexico-grammatical phrases and discourse expressions in which conventional deictic markers (e.g. pronominals) partake to force conceptual operations (such as the ODC–IDC movement). An example of the proximization approach to deixis is Cap's (2013) spatial proximization framework (see Table 2.1), which not only reflects the constituents and the mechanism of proximization in DS,

Table 2.1 Spatial proximization framework and its key lexico-grammatical items

Category	Key items
1. (Noun phrases (NPs) construed as elements of the deictic centre of the DS (IDCs))	['USA', 'United States', 'America']; ['American people', 'Americans', 'our people/nation/country/society']; ['free people/nations/countries/societies/ world']; ['democratic people/nations/ countries/societies/world']
2. (NPs construed as elements outside the deictic centre of the DS (ODCs))	['Iraq', 'Saddam Hussein', 'Saddam', 'Hussein']; ['Iraqi regime/dictatorship']; ['terrorists']; ['terrorist organizations/ networks', 'Al-Qaeda']; ['extremists/ radicals']; ['foreign regimes/dictatorships']
3. (Verb phrases (VPs) of motion and directionality construed as markers of movement of ODCs towards the deictic centre)	['are determined/intend to seek/acquire WMD']; ['might/may/could/can use WMD against *an IDC*']; ['expand/grow *in military capacity that could be directed against an IDC*']; ['move/are moving/ head/are heading/have set their course towards confrontation *with an IDC* ']
4. (VPs of action construed as markers of impact of ODCs upon IDCs)	['destroy *an IDC*']; ['set aflame/burn down *an IDC or IDC values*']
5. (NPs denoting abstract concepts construed as anticipations of impact of ODCs upon IDCs)	['threat']; ['danger']
6. (NPs denoting abstract concepts construed as effects of impact of ODCs upon IDCs)	['catastrophe']; ['tragedy']

but also serves to abstract the relevant lexico-grammatical items. The items in the framework are quantifiable, which means they define the intensity of the kind of proximization applied. Table 2.1 below includes the spatial items abstracted from a corpus of the US anti-terrorist rhetoric – a state interventionist discourse widely analysed within the proximization paradigm (Cap 2013; among others).

The six categories depicted in the left-hand column are a stable element of the spatial proximization framework, while the key items provided in the right-hand column depend on the actual discourse under investigation. Table 2.1 includes the most frequent of the spatial proximization items in the 2001–2010 corpus of presidential addresses on the US anti-terrorist policies.[1] Quantifiable items appear in square brackets and include combinations of words separated by slashes with the head word. For example, the item ['free people/nations/countries/societies/world'] includes the following combinations, all of which contribute to the general count of the first category: 'free people', 'free nations', 'free countries', 'free societies', 'free world'. The italicized phrases indicate parts that allow synonymous phrases to fill in the item and thus increase its count. For example, the item ['destroy *an IDC*'] in category 4 subsumes several quantifiable variations, such as 'destroy America', 'destroy our land' or 'destroy the free and democratic world'.[2]

The framework and its 6 categories capture not only the initial arrangement of the DS (ctg. 1, 2), but also (and crucially) the shift leading to the ODC–IDC clash (3, 4) and the (anticipated) effects of the clash (5, 6). The third category, central to the design of the framework, sets 'traditional' deictic expressions such as personal pronouns to work *pragmatically* together with the other elements of the superordinate VP. As a result, the VP acquires a deictic status, in the sense that on top of conventionally denoting static DS entities (marked by pronominals), it also helps index a more challenging element of context, their movement, which establishes the target perspective construed by the speaker.

Emerging from the spatial proximization framework (as well as the temporal and axiological frameworks [Cap 2013]) is the (ii) lexico-grammatical contribution of the STA model. The model makes it possible to extract *quantifiable* linguistic evidence of the use of different proximization strategies within a specific timeframe. The STA model can thus also account quantitatively for cases where for contextual reasons one proximization strategy is dropped and replaced by another.

A Case Study of Proximization in (State) Political Discourse

As has been mentioned, the main application of PT so far has been to critical studies of state political discourses seeking legitimization of interventionist preventive measures against an external threat. In this section we exemplify this application, discussing instances of the US discourse of the War on Terror. Specifically, we outline what proximization strategies were used to legitimize the US government's decision to go to war in Iraq (March 2003), and what adjustments in the use of the strategies were made later (from November 2003) as a result of contextual changes which took place in the meantime.

Initiating Legitimization Through Proximization

Below we look at parts of G.W. Bush's speech at the American Enterprise Institute (AEI), which was delivered on 26 February 2003.[3] The speech took place only three weeks before the first US and coalition troops entered Iraq on March 19, and has often been considered (e.g. Silberstein 2004) a manifesto of the Iraq war. The goal of the speech was to list direct reasons for the intervention, while also locating it in the global context of the War on Terror declared by G.W. Bush on the night of the 9/11 attacks. The realization of this goal involved a strategic use of various lexico-grammatical forms reflecting different proximization strategies.

Providing his rationale for war, President Bush had to confront the kind of public reluctance faced by many of his White House predecessors: how to legitimize the US involvement in military action in a far-away place, among a far-away people, of whom the American people knew little (Bacevich 2010). The AEI speech is remarkable in its consistent continuity of attempts to overcome this reluctance. It amply applies spatio-temporal and axiological proximization strategies, which are performed in diligently designed pragmatic patterns drawing from more general conceptual premises for legitimization:

We are facing a crucial period in the history of our nation, and of the civilized world.... On a September morning, threats that had gathered for years, in secret and far away, led to murder in our country on a massive scale. As a result, we must look at security in a new way, because our country is a battlefield in the first war of the 21st century.... We learned a lesson: the dangers of our time must be confronted actively and forcefully, before we see them again in our skies and our cities. And we will not allow the flames of hatred and violence in the affairs of men.... The world has a clear interest in the spread of democratic values, because stable and free nations do not breed the ideologies of murder.... Saddam Hussein and his weapons of mass destruction are a direct threat to our people and to all free people.... My job is to protect the American people. When it comes to our security and freedom, we really don't need anybody's permission.... We've tried diplomacy for 12 years. It hasn't worked. Saddam Hussein hasn't disarmed, he's armed. Today the goal is to remove the Iraqi regime and to rid Iraq of weapons of mass destruction.... The liberation of millions is the fulfillment of America's founding promise. The objectives we've set in this war are worthy of America, worthy of all the acts of heroism and generosity that have come before.

In a nutshell, the AEI speech states that there are WMD[4] in Iraq and that, given historical context and experience, ideological characteristics of the adversary as opposed to American values and national legacy, and G. W. Bush's obligations as standing US president, there is a case for legitimate military intervention. This complex picture involves historical flashbacks, as well as descriptions of the current situation, which both engage proximization strategies. These strategies, involving the usual credibility ploys (cf. Chap. 1), operate at two interrelated levels, which can be described as 'diachronic' and 'synchronic'. At the diachronic level, Bush evokes ideological representations of the remote past, which are 'proximized' to underline the continuity and steadfastness of purpose, thus linking with and sanctioning current actions as acts of faithfulness to long-accepted principles and values. An example is the final part: 'The liberation is . . . promise. The objectives . . . have come before'. It launches a temporal analogy 'axis' which links a past reference point (the founding of America) with the present point, creating a common conceptual space for both the proximized historical 'acts of heroism' and the current and/ or prospective acts construed as their natural 'follow-ups'. This kind of legitimization, performed by mostly temporal and axiological proximiza- tion (the originally past values become the 'here and now' premises for action[5]), draws, in many ways, upon the socio-psychological predisposi- tions of the US addressee (Dunmire 2011). On the lexical plane, the job of establishing the past-present link is performed by assertions, which fall within addressee's 'latitude of acceptance' (Jowett and O'Donnell 1992).[6] The assertions range from indisputably acceptable ('My job is . . .'; 'The liberation of millions . . .'), to acceptable due to credibility developed progressively within a 'fact-belief series' ('We've tried diplo- macy for twelve years [FACT] . . . he's armed [BELIEF]'), but none of them is inconsistent with the key predispositions of the addressee.

At the synchronic level, historical flashbacks are not completely aban- doned, but they involve proximization of *near* history and the main legitimization premise is not (continuing) ideological commitments, but the *direct physical threats* looming over the country ('a battlefield', in G.W. Bush's words). As the threats require a swift and strong pre-emptive response, the 'default' proximization strategy operating at the synchronic level is spatial proximization, often featuring a temporal element. Its task is to raise fears of imminence of the threat, which might be 'external' and 'distant' apparently, but in fact able to materialize anytime. The lexico-grammatical carriers of the spatial proximization include such items and phrases as 'secret and far away', 'all free people', 'stable and free nations', 'Saddam Hussein and his weapons of mass destruction', etc., which force dichotomous, 'good against evil' representations of the IDCs (America, Western [free, democratic] world) and the ODCs (Saddam Hussein, Iraqi regime, terrorists), located at a relative distance from each other. This geographical and geopolitical distance is symbolically construed as shrinking, as, on the one hand, the ODC entities cross the DS towards its deictic centre and, on the other, the centre (IDC) entities declare a reaction. The ODC shift is enacted by forced inference and metaphorization. The inference involves an analogy to 9/11 ('On a September morning ... '), whereby the event stage is construed as facing another physical impact, whose ('current') consequences are scrupulously described ('before we see them [flames] again in our skies and our cities').

While all spatial proximization in the text draws upon the presumed WMD presence in Iraq – and its potential availability to terrorists for acts far more destructive than the 9/11 attacks – Bush does not disregard the possibility of having to resort to an alternative rationale for war in the future. Consequently, the speech contains 'supporting' ideological premises, however tied to the principal premise. An example is the use of axiological proximization in 'The world has a clear interest in the spread of democratic values, because stable and free nations do not breed the ideologies of murder'. This ideological argument is not synonymous with Bush's proximization of remote history we have seen before, as its current line subsumes acts of the adversary rather than his/America's own acts. As such it involves a more typical axiological proximization, where the initially ideological conflict turns, over time, into a physical clash. Notably, in its ideological-physical duality it forces a spectrum of speculations over whether the current threat is 'still' ideological or 'already' physical. Since any result of these speculations can be effectively cancelled in a prospective discourse, the example quoted ('The world ... ') points towards a relation between proximization and implicature (cf. Chap. 1).

Maintaining Legitimization Through Adjustments in Proximization Strategies

Political legitimization pursued in temporally extensive contexts – such as the timeframe of the Iraq war – often involves redefinition of the initial legitimization premises and coercion patterns and proximization is very well suited to enact these redefinitions in discourse. The legitimization obtained in the AEI speech and how the unfolding geopolitical context has put it to test is an illuminating case in point. Let us repeat that although President Bush has made the WMD the central premise for the Iraq war, he has left half-open an 'emergency door' to be able to reach for an alternative rationale. Come November 2003 (the mere eight months into the Iraq war), and Bush's pro-war rhetoric adopts (or rather has to adopt) such an emergency alternative rationale, as it becomes evident that there have never been weapons of mass destruction in Iraq, at least not in the ready-to-use product sense. The change of G.W. Bush's stance consists in a swift move from strong fear appeals involving a 'direct threat' to a more subtle ideological argument for legitimization, based on axiological proximization. This change can be seen in the Whitehall Palace address of November 19:

> By advancing freedom in the greater Middle East, we help end a cycle of dictatorship and radicalism that brings millions of people to misery and brings danger to our own people. By struggling for justice in Iraq, Burma, in Sudan, and in Zimbabwe, we give hope to suffering people and improve the chances for stability and progress. Had we failed to act, the dictator's programs for weapons of mass destruction would continue to this day. Had we failed to act, Iraq's torture chambers would still be filled with victims, terrified and innocent.... For all who love freedom and peace, the world without Saddam Hussein's regime is a better and safer place.

The now dominant axiological proximization involves a dense concentration of ideological and value-oriented lexical items (e.g. 'freedom', 'justice', 'stability', 'progress', 'peace' vs. 'dictatorship', 'radicalism') as well as of items/phrases indicating the human dimension of the conflict ('misery', 'suffering people', 'terrified victims' vs. 'the world' [being] 'a better and safer place'). All of these lexico-grammatical forms serve to build, as in the case of the AEI address, dichotomous representations of the DS 'home' and 'peripheral/adversarial' entities (IDCs vs. ODCs), and the representation of impact upon the DS 'home' entities (cf. Fig. 2.1). In contrast to the AEI speech, however, all the entities (both IDCs and ODCs) are construed in abstract, rather than physical, 'tangible' terms, as respective lexical items are not explicitly but only inferentially attributed to concrete parties/groups. For example, compare phrases such as 'all free people', 'stable and free nations', [terrorist] 'flames of hatred', etc., in the AEI address, with the single-word abstract items of general reference such as 'dictatorship' and 'radicalism', in the Whitehall speech. Apparently, proximization in the Whitehall speech is essentially a proximization of antagonistic values, and not so much of physical entities as embodiments of these values. The consequences for maintaining legitimization stance which began with the AEI address are enormous.

First, there is no longer a commitment to a material threat posed by a physical entity. Second, the relief of this commitment does not completely disqualify the original WMD premise, as the antagonistic 'peripheral' values retain a capacity to materialize within the DS deictic centre (viz. '...a cycle of dictatorship and radicalism that brings millions of people to misery and brings danger to our own people', reiterating 'The world has a clear interest in the spread of democratic values, because stable and free nations do not breed the ideologies of murder' from the AEI speech). Third, as the nature of ideological principles is such that they are (considered) global or broadly shared, the socio-ideological argument helps extend the spectrum of the US (military) engagement ('Burma', 'Sudan', 'Zimbabwe'), which in turn forces the construal of failure to detect WMD in Iraq as merely an unlucky incident amongst other (successful) operations, and not as something that could potentially ruin the US credibility.

Add to these general factors the power of legitimization ploys in specific pragmalinguistic constructs ('programs for weapons of mass destruction',[7] the enumeration of the 'new' foreign fields of engagement [viz. 'Burma', etc., above], the always effective appeals for solidarity in compassion [viz. 'terrified victims' in 'torture chambers']) and there are reasons to conclude that the autumn 2003 change to essentially axiological discourse (subsuming axiological proximization) has helped a lot towards saving credibility and thus maintaining legitimization of not only the Iraq war, but the later anti-terrorist campaigns as well. The flexible interplay and the discursive switches between spatial and axiological proximization (both aided by temporal projections) in the early stages of the US anti-terrorist policy rhetoric have indeed made a major contribution.

Towards Further Applications

Drawing on the cognitive-linguistic approach to discourse, PT provides the cognitive representation of DS with a dynamic element reflecting speaker's awareness of the constantly evolving context. In its account of discourse dynamics, PT focuses on the strategic, ideological and goal-oriented essence of construals of the near and the remote. Most importantly, it focuses on how the imagining of the closeness and remoteness, a core element of conceptualization (cf. Chap. 1), can be manipulated in the public/political sphere and bound up with fear, security and conflict. PT is thus a critically minded revision of the classical models of DS such as Chilton's DST or Levinson's spatio-temporal frames of reference. It is also a truly *linguistic* revision, in terms of linking specific construals to stable and recurrent sets of lexico-grammatical items (cf. Table 2.1). As such, PT is ideally suited to analyse discursive representations of legitimization, delegitimization, coercion and other socially consequential phenomena involving a threat element.

Given its broad conceptual framework, PT possesses explanatory power reaching far beyond state political discourse. The last thirty years have seen prolific discourse studies in the most urgent social issues such as racism, xenophobia, national identity, gender identity, equality and inequality, social exclusion and many more. This list, by no means exhaustive, gives a sense of the spectrum of discourses where proximization applies. The main focus of contemporary discourse analysis (practiced mostly under the 'critical' banner[8]) is on the many strategies in which worldviews, ideologies and identities are reflected, (re)-enacted, negotiated, modified, reproduced, etc., in discourse. This calls for an analytic framework able to capture the original status of the different worldviews, ideologies and identities, as well as the 'target status', that is the *change* the analyst claims is taking place through the speaker's *use* of discourse. As a theory of conceptual organization as well as re-organization of the DS (cf. Fig. 2.1), Proximization seems the natural candidate.

In the next four chapters, PT is used to explore four public discourses: health, environment, modern technology and (anti-)migration. We argue that these seemingly different discourses are remarkably similar in their consistent use of the threat element as the central premise for legitimization. We thus claim that threat construction is a core feature of public communication, which relies for policy-making and policy legitimization on the discursively construed aura of fear and general anxiety. As a linguistically minded theory,

Proximization brings to light the specific, lexico-grammatical choices responsible for threat construction and fear generation. In so doing, it provides CDA and other critical and sociological approaches with an organized empirical model to add to their formative conceptual frameworks. It binds together the main concepts – legitimization, credibility, coercion – and sets them in relation to general cognitive underpinnings of communication, such as indexing, polarization and fear of the remote.

NOTES

1. The corpus contains 402 texts (601,856 words) of *speeches and remarks*, downloaded from the White House website http://www.whitehouse.gov in January 2011. It includes texts matching at least two of the three issue tags: *defense, foreign policy, homeland security*.
2. See Cap (2013, pp. 108–109) for details. See also the two other frameworks, temporal (p. 116) and axiological (p. 122), which we do not have space to discuss here.
3. The parts are quoted according to the chronology of the speech.
4. Weapons of mass destruction.
5. This is a secondary variant of axiological proximization. As will be shown, axiological proximization mostly involves the adversary (ODC); antagonistic values are 'dormant' triggers for a possible ODC impact.
6. We have noted in Chap. 1 that the best credibility and thus legitimization effects can be expected if the speaker produces her message in line with the psychological, social, political, cultural, etc., predispositions of the addressee. However, since a full compliance is almost never possible, it is essential that a novel message is at least tentatively or partly acceptable; then, its acceptability and the speaker's credibility tend to increase over time.
7. The nominal phrase '[Iraq's] programs for WMD' is essentially an implicature able to legitimize, in response to contextual needs, any of the following inferences: 'Iraq possesses WMD', 'Iraq is developing WMD', 'Iraq intends to develop WMD', 'Iraq intended to develop WMD', and more. The phrase was among G.W. Bush's rhetorical favourites in later stages of the Iraq war, when the original premises for war were called into question.
8. See Hart and Cap (2014) for an overview of current work in Critical Discourse Analysis (CDA).

CHAPTER 3

Health Discourse:
The War on Cancer and Beyond

Abstract Initiating a series of four case studies, this chapter explores the applicability of Proximization Theory in health discourse. It demonstrates that fear-inducing proximization strategies are widely present in the discourse of disease prevention and health promotion. Picturing disease as 'aggressive enemy' which 'invades' the patient, the speaker (medical practitioner, healthcare institution) generates a fear appeal which helps justification of a preferred course of treatment. The chapter uses data from anti-tobacco and swine flu prevention campaigns.

Keywords Health discourse · War on cancer · Cancer prevention discourse · Anti-tobacco discourse

The study in Chap. 2, as well as several other proximization studies (e.g. Cap 2013; Dunmire 2011; Hart 2010, 2014; Wieczorek 2013), points towards new empirical territories. They suggest that the explanatory power of Proximization Theory (PT) goes beyond state political discourse (such as the US anti-terrorist rhetoric) and can be used to account for a broader range of legitimization discourses in the vast space of public communication. Prospects look promising as many of these discourses demonstrate analogies, apparently remote yet actually close, to state-level interventionist discourse. First, many reveal a similar conceptual groundwork, that is the presumed cognitive dichotomy of the 'bad Other' encroaching upon the 'good Self'.

P. Cap, *The Language of Fear*, DOI 10.1057/978-1-137-59731-1_3

29

Second, many demonstrate a common pragmatic function, that is soliciting approval of (radical) measures to offset the growing threat. As such, public discourse emerges as very strongly dependent on threat construction and threat proximization for effective policy-making and, above all, policy communication. This can be evidenced in formal lexico-grammatical terms by PT. Our initial focus is on health discourse and cancer prevention discourse in particular, though we also include examples from other domains.

PROXIMIZATION OF THREAT IN CANCER PREVENTION DISCOURSE

The War on Cancer Scenario

The discourse of cancer prevention involves a strategic use of fear appeals, drawing on metaphoric construals of an *enemy* entity (cancer) posing an *imminent threat of impact* on the *home* entity (patient). In response, the patient and her healthcare team wage a 'war on cancer', which is often a *preventive* kind of war. Although, as will be argued, the construals underlying the war on cancer metaphor are not entirely synonymous with the proximization construals in state interventionist discourse, there is still enough similarity to consider the discourse of cancer prevention a field to be explored by PT.

The war metaphor has been the prevailing metaphor used to describe and 'combat' cancer since at least 1971, when US President Richard M. Nixon declared a federal 'war on cancer' with the National Cancer Act. Following this legislation, as well as Sontag's (1978) seminal book *Illness as Metaphor*, medical discourse, both in and outside the US, has quickly implemented the concept, adding the war on cancer metaphor to an already rich inventory of metaphors involving 'wars' on other negative social phenomena, such as drugs, poverty or illiteracy.

Van Rijn-van Tongeren (1997) claims that the concepts of war and cancer reveal a perfect metaphoric correspondence: there is an enemy (the cancer), a commander (the physician), a combatant (the patient), allies (the medical team), as well as formidable weaponry (chemical, biological and nuclear weapons, at the disposal of the medical team). Another analogy, she argues, is that both concepts connote 'an unmistakable seriousness of purpose' (Van Rijn-van Tongeren 1997, p. 46). Based on these observations, she describes the 'war on cancer' in terms of the following conceptual scenario:

(1) Cancer is an *aggressive enemy* that *invades* the body. In response, the body *launches an offensive* and *defends* itself, *fighting* back with its *army of*

killer T-cells. However, this is not enough and doctors are needed to *target, attack* and try to *defeat, destroy, kill* or *wipe out* the cancer cells with their *arsenal* of *lethal weapons.* However, cancer cells may become *resistant* and more specialised treatments are required, such as *magic bullets* or *stealth viruses.* (Van Rijn-van Tongeren 1997, emphasis original)

The consecutive stages of the scenario are widely represented in real-life discourse. Van Rijn-van Tongeren (1997) gives, among many others, the following examples (emphasis original). Van Rijn-van Tongeren's data come generally from academic publications, such as monographs, text-books and articles (examples [3–5]), but also bulletins and newspaper articles aimed at a broad public (example [2]).

(2) The next trial involves several hundred patients, helping microwaves become another *cancer-fighting tool.*
(3) This molecule called Sumo, is then *attacked* by an enzyme called RNF4, a process that also *destroys* the cancer-causing proteins.
(4) A second gene, called LMTK2 is a promising *target* for new drugs to treat the disease.
(5) This activates only those antibodies surrounding cancer, which then attract the immune system's *army of killer T cells,* to *destroy* the tumor.

Van Rijn-van Tongeren's scenario, as well as the examples, rings some familiar notes. Like in the proximization arrangement of political interventionist discourse, there is an 'alien' entity ready to invade (or actually invading) the 'home' entity, that is, here, the body of the patient. The 'alien' entity is construed as evil and actively operating ('aggressive enemy'), thus the impact probability is high. The 'home' entity has the capacity to deliver a counter-strike, which is defensive/neutralizing, as much as offensive/preventive in character ('the body *launches an offensive* and *defends* itself, *fighting* back with its *army of killer T-cells*'). These analogies prove that, in its basic conceptual design, the discourse of cancer prevention and treatment borrows from state interventionist rhetoric a lot. Of course, there is never a full correspondence. The 'alien' entity cannot be described as a genuinely 'external' entity (ODC), since cancer cells develop inside of the patient's body. Furthermore, the body is not, technically, the only 'home' or 'Self' entity (IDC) that counters the 'alien'/'Other' entity, since its *'army of T-cells'* gets support (medical treatment) from another party (the physician), which the latter has not been 'invaded'. These and other differences call for a more extensive, textual look at the cancer prevention discourse, to distinguish the areas which can be described in terms of the STA model, from those which might not be describable quite as easily, unless the model is revised to deal with a broader spectrum of data.

A Proximization Analysis of the Rhetoric of Cancer Prevention

The following text appeared in the spring 2011 edition of the Newsletter of the British Association of Cancer Research (BACR). Its argument, structure and lexical choices seem all quite representative of the contemporary discourse of cancer prevention and treatment, both specialized and popular (cf. Semino 2008, pp. 11–12):

> (6) Some say we can contain melanoma with standard chemotherapy measures. The evidence we have says we must strike it with a full force in its earliest stages. We will continue to conduct screening programmes to spot the deadly disease before it has spread throughout the body. We must be able to wipe out all the infected cells in one strike, otherwise it takes a moment before they continue to replicate and migrate around the body. We now aim to develop a new treatment that targets the infected cells with precision, effectively destroying the engine at the heart of the disease, and doing minimal harm to healthy cells. We will inject specially-designed antibodies coated in a light-sensitive shell. The coating prevents the antibodies from causing a massive immune reaction throughout the body. Once the 'cloaked' antibodies have been injected, we will shine the new strong ultraviolet light on the engine and the infected cells.

To elucidate all analogies and empirical similarities, the analysis of this text in terms of PT and the STA model must involve, same as the analysis of the US anti-terrorist discourse in Chap. 2, at least three interrelated levels. These are: the conceptual level of organization of the Discourse Space (DS), the level of lexis responsible for the enactment of strategic changes to the DS principal organization, and finally the coercion level, where the text is considered an example of legitimization discourse which aims to win support for specific actions performed by the speaker. At the DS conceptual level, we must be able to determine the presence of the IDC ('home', 'central', 'Self') entity and the ODC ('alien', 'peripheral', 'Other') entity, the existence of a conceptual shift whereby the ODC entity impacts the IDC entity, and a preventive or reactive posture of the IDC entity. Looking at (8), this arrangement indeed holds in general, though there are some deviations. The IDC status can be assigned, most directly, to the patient's body, which is invaded by cancer cells, which thus emerge as the ODC entity. This basic proximization construal follows the standard metaphoric conceptualization of the body as a container (Lakoff and Johnson 1980; etc.). But the container metaphor is only partly of relevance here since the patient's body is not a typical IDC, in the sense of where the impact it undergoes comes from. In that sense, the cancer cells, responsible for the impact, are not a typical ODC, either. As has been pointed out, cancer cells develop, technically, *inside* the patient's body. At the same time, *causes* of cancer are put down to internal (e.g. genetic), as well as external (e.g. civilizational), factors. The picture gets even more complex if we consider the aspect of agency. While the body has an internal defense mechanism, fighting the cancer cells involves mostly external resources, that is measures applied by the physician. Thus, in terms of neutralization of the ODC impact, the physician becomes an IDC entity as well, and even more so considering he remains under the cancer *threat* himself. What we arrive at, then, is a rather broad concept of the IDC entity, involving the patient and, by the attribution of agency and the recognition of common threat, the physician, as well as a vaguely construed concept of the ODC party, involving the infected cells in the patient, but also a whole array of cancer provoking factors, 'located' externally. Looking at (6), it appears that the only (though crucial) part of the default proximization arrangement that cancer discourse does not alter in any way is the construal of the very impact. Indeed, it seems that all of its characteristics, like speed, imminence and deadliness, are there in the text, which in that sense resembles the two texts of state political discourse in Chap. 2.

This last observation explains why there are fewer analytic problems at the level of lexis. In proximization discourse, lexical markers of the ODC *impact* generally count among the most plentiful, within all the linguistic material categorized (Cap 2013). As a result, the abundance of such markers in (6) makes its phrases resemble many of the discourse items and sequences we have seen above in the war on terror rhetoric.[1] The ODC impact speed is coded explicitly in phrases such as '*spread through- out* the body', 'it takes *a moment*', 'replicate and migrate around', and can also be inferred from 'we must strike it with a full force *in its earliest stages*', 'we must be able to wipe out all the infected cells *in one strike*' and '*the engine* at the heart of the disease'. The imminence is construed in, for instance, 'before it has spread throughout' and 'in its earliest stages', presuppositions of the ODC's inevitably fast growth. The effects of the impact are explicitly marked by the 'deadly disease' phrase.

At the coercion-legitimization level, the STA model recognizes in (6) an attempt to solicit legitimization of a non-standard course of treatment, sanctioned by the momentousness of the decision-making context ('We *now* aim'), as well as by the clear evidence the speaker possesses ('The evidence we have says') which speaks in favour of the treatment. Since the legitimization is sought by the physician acting, in a way, 'on behalf of' the patient, and not by the patient herself, we again face the problem of who, under the current design of the STA model, belongs to the deictic centre and who, thus, is acting (or is supposed to act) in response to the ODC threat. The recurrence of this issue at the coercion-legitimization level of analysis of cancer discourse delineates a possible avenue for the modification of selected structural elements of PT (as in Cap 2013), to better process data beyond the state-political interventionist discourse. Apparently, PT may be in need of a critical reflection on the size and range of the DS and its deictic centre in proximization operations.

It is not our ambition at this point to develop this diagnosis into a full-length methodological discussion. Given the goals of the present book, the current PT offers enough to capture the role of the threat element in legitimization strategies of health discourse. Crucially, proximization analysis demonstrates a consistent reliance of health discourse and disease prevention discourse in particular on three interrelated threat construals: *the construal of the ODC as an enemy entity, the construal of the ODC impact speed* and *the construal of the ODC impact consequences.* These three construals underlie cancer prevention discourse as well as a number of other discourses in the field of (preventive) medicine.

Beyond the War on Cancer

The following two texts (7–8) are concerned with different health issues, communicated by different institutional speakers to different audiences, via different news channels in different media cultures. They are however remarkably similar in their consistent use of threat-based strategies in the service of legitimization and public mobilization. Most of these strategies involve spatial as well as temporal proximization.

(7) H1N1 virus returns, already claiming lives of 10 British adults

The swine flu virus that swept the world last year causing a global health emergency has returned to claim the lives of 10 adults in the UK in the past six weeks. The 10 deaths were in younger adults under 65 and directly associated with H1N1 swine flu. Only 3 had underlying conditions, the rest were healthy before being struck down by the killer virus, according to the Health Protection Agency (HPA). Seasonal flu normally causes severe illness in the elderly. The H1N1 swine flu virus is now targeting pregnant women, younger adults, and those with chronic conditions, making it a cause of particular alarm. No other similar reports of deaths linked with swine flu have been received from elsewhere in Europe. Official figures show GP consultations for flu-like illness in England were at 13.3 per 100,000 population last week, well below baseline levels. 'We are just beginning to see more of H1N1 activity in the UK', said John Watson, head of respiratory diseases at the Health Protection Agency. The fear among flu experts is that the deadly virus could mutate to cause more severe illness in younger adults. The NHS recommends people have the 2014 seasonal flu vaccination to protect them against swine flu.

(The Independent, 20 January 2014)

(8) Secondhand smoke could penetrate your body in no time at all. The moment you inhale your lungs and blood become affected, transmitting toxicants all over your brain, heart, stomach . . . , your neural, respiratory, cardiovascular . . . systems. Toxicity is growing every second you are exposed, increasing the chances of stroke, heart attack, cancer, . . . affecting reproductive capacity in both males and females. . . . Until all forms of public smoking are banned state-wide in California, your life is at a continual risk. . . .

Tobacco kills, and people who market it are terrorists. The bomb is ticking. Will we respond? If we don't, who will? Awareness is not enough; only strategic action will change the course of human events. The industry is increasingly spending money to target all, but especially the most vulnerable cells of our society: children, minorities, and American citizens who had immigrated to our country from the third world. . . . We need to more aggressively fight tobacco marketing. This is an issue of social justice. Predatory marketing by the tobacco industry must be actively opposed.

(Action on Smoking and Health in California, Internet release on passive smoking and tobacco marketing, 29 July 2009)

The strategies of threat construction in (7) and (8) involve a concerted interplay of construals of the enemy entity (ODC), its ability to produce quick impact, and the (destructive) effects of that impact. Although the two texts differ with regard to the kind and number of ODC agents ('swine flu virus' in [7]; 'secondhand smoke', 'tobacco', 'tobacco industry' in [10]), both construe all the ODC agents as inherently evil ('killer virus', 'deadly virus', 'tobacco kills' '[tobacco industry] are terrorists'). This is contrasted with the innocence and helplessness of the victims: both texts include in the IDC group the most vulnerable individuals, such as 'pregnant women' and 'the elderly' in (7), and 'children' in (8). As a result, the fear-raising appeal of the enemy entity gets stronger, triggering expectations of an effective defense or prevention plan. The characterization of the ODC entity as evil is deftly combined with its construal as active and potent. In (7) a historical flashback is used to endorse the high calibre of the current threat ('The swine flu virus that swept the world last year causing a global health emergency has returned'). In (8), a bomb metaphor is used to underline the size and urgency of the threat ('The bomb is ticking').

This brings us to the construal of the ODC impact. To force the construal of the impact as a close and threatening possibility, both (7) and (8) include expressions structured grammatically in the progressive imperfective aspect ('The H1N1 swine flu virus is targeting', 'We are just beginning to see more of H1N1 activity', 'Toxicity is growing every second', 'The bomb is ticking'). It is commonly accepted that with regard to its grammatical and discourse function, the progressive imperfective represents actions as 'unbounded', incomplete and without explicitly indicated endpoints (Bybee and Fleischman 1995). It thus helps construe the present moment as durative, that is continuing on into the future unless intervened upon. The continuity salient in the progressive imperfective phrases can thus be read, in our case, as the continuity of threat extending into the future yet without indication of the precise moment of materialization. The consequences of such a construal for fear generation are enormous. First, the threat that is unpredictable gets automatically bigger, entailing a continual mobilization and preparedness of resources to handle it. Second, since the timeframe of 'waiting for the threat to happen' is extensive, it provides a background against which the actual materialization of the threat (the actual impact) is conceptualized. In this process, the impact is naturally construed as a 'deadly strike', a nick of time bringing about devastating and irreversible change.

The last element of the arrangement is the construal of the ODC impact effects. Since the ultimate goal of (7) and (8) is unconditional legitimization, and legitimization gains are the greatest when the impact of ODCs is conceptualized as maximally consequential, the two texts feature a number of constructs which evoke globality of the gathering threat, as well as a potentially massive toll it could take if unstopped. The items/phrases construing the range of the threat include 'swept the *world*', '*global* health emergency', 'in *both males and females*', 'target *all*' and 'our society'. Apart from these nominal phrases that extend the calibre/target of the threat, several verb phrases (VPs) are used (such as 'could mutate') to multiply its sources. The possible toll of the threat is described as huge and heavy ('deadly virus', 'toxicants all over', 'life (...) at a continual risk'), thus calling for and justifying radical measures ('aggressively fight tobacco marketing', 'must be actively opposed').

In general, the coercion and legitimization strategies in (7) and (8) are realized in spatio-temporal construals which depict and proximize the threat element as a real, 'tangible' entity. This is no surprise given the overarching legitimization goals, which involve quick and unequivocal approval of the proposed course of action. It seems that the same rule holds for most of health discourse and disease prevention discourse in particular. Naturally enough, speakers in health discourse aim at an unconditional and, above all, ultra-fast legitimization, in order to be able to take rapid actions against equally rapid negative developments. Possessing a uniquely high capacity for threat construction and fear generation, spatio-temporal proximization strategies seem to make the best rhetorical choice.

Health Discourse and PT

This chapter has made the first attempt to redirect the empirical focus of PT, from its 'cradle' domain of state political discourse, towards the vast and heterogeneous territory of 'public discourse' in general. What have we learnt about, first, the conceptual characteristics of threat and fear generation patterns in health discourse compared to political discourse? And what can be said, as a result, about the compatibility of PT to handle further interventionist discourses in the public domain? To receive an answer, we re-focus on example (8), which we re-quote in two parts (8a–8b) below:

(8a) Secondhand smoke could penetrate your body in no time at all. The moment you inhale your lungs and blood become affected, transmitting toxicants all over your brain, heart, stomach..., your neural, respiratory, cardiovascular...systems. Toxicity is growing every second you are exposed, increasing the chances of stroke, heart attack, cancer,...affecting

reproductive capacity in both males and females. . . . Until all forms of public smoking are banned state-wide in California, your life is at a continual risk. . . .
(8b) Tobacco kills, and people who market it are terrorists. The bomb is ticking. Will we respond? If we don't, who will? Awareness is not enough; only strategic action will change the course of human events. The industry is increasingly spending money to target all, but especially the most vulnerable cells of our society: children, minorities, and American citizens who had immigrated to our country from the third world. . . . We need to more aggressively fight tobacco marketing. This is an issue of social justice. Predatory marketing by the tobacco industry must be actively opposed.
(Action on Smoking and Health in California, Internet release on passive smoking and tobacco marketing, 29 July 2009)

The division of excerpt (8) into two parts (8a–8b) allows examination of the conceptual specificity and heterogeneity of health discourse, particularly disease prevention discourse. Even though (8a) and (8b) belong to the same text, they reveal, apart from similarities, some subtle differences with regard to the arrangement of the DS which they construe to generate threat and fear. Both (8a) and (8b) make use of proximization strategies conceptually similar to those in the 'canonical' representation of state political discourse (except that the response they legitimize comes no longer from the speaker alone but rather from the speaker and the addressee together). At the DS basic organization level, in both parts the speaker and the addressee are positioned in the deictic centre, facing an external threat entity construed as moving from the apparent periphery of the DS in the direction of the DS centre. Yet in contrast to these similarities, the argument in (8a) differs from (8b), as well as from a 'typical' proximization discourse, in its use of intended vagueness. The passive voice makes it unclear who exactly is expected to act. At the same time, the addressee in (8b) seems more concrete (activists, voters, legislators) and more able to deliver a response ('Will we respond? If we don't, who will?'). (8b) uses mostly active voice, as well as inclusive 'we', which refers to a broad range of possible agents.

Less vagueness can be observed as regards the ODC entities, which become proximized to negatively affect the DS central entities (IDCs). However, the overall design of the DS is again not quite uniform. In (8a) the ODC entity is simply 'secondhand smoke', which is construed as animate, almost 'intelligent' in fact. This not only maximizes the speed and force of the impact, but also marks its 'strategic' character, which involves a step-by-step assumption of full control over the body. Speaking of 'the body', we must note that the IDCs in (8a) are not only the persons exposed to secondhand smoke within their social space, but also their organs, exposed to the smoke within the bodies, conceptualized as 'containers' similar to social spaces. This onion structure of the DS 'Self' entities does not detract from their general status as 'central'; it only produces some referential and agency problems. That is, while the collective agency in (8a) can easily pertain to people, it cannot pertain to their organs. In (8b) the ODC entity is again the smoke (tobacco), but also the 'tobacco industry' and 'people who market it'. In contrast to (8a), (8b) reveals no vagueness resulting from the IDC composition.

At the level of lexis responsible for the discourse enactment of proximization there are fewer asymmetries. In both (8a) and (8b) some strongly appealing lexico-grammatical forms are used ('Tobacco kills, and people who market it are terrorists. The bomb is ticking', '...to target all, but especially the most vulnerable cells of our society...', 'Predatory marketing...', '...could penetrate...in no time at all. The moment you inhale your...become affected, transmitting...all over...', 'Toxicity is growing every second...', '...stroke, heart attack, cancer...', '...life is at a continual risk'), to indicate the ODC 'evil' power, capacity and unpredictability such as necessary to force construals of the continuing possibility of an unexpected, fast and devastating impact (note the metaphor of terrorist attacks). At the coercion level, the analogies to state political discourse are equally clear, involving a consistent use of proximization strategies in the service of legitimization. Both (8a) and (8b) include discourse that works consistently towards legitimization of the adoption of anti-tobacco policies – even though there are some differences with regard to who is directly addressed, who is expected to respond, and who has the necessary tools. The similarities at the coercion and lexico-grammatical levels seem to offset these relatively small disanalogies at the DS organization level. We can thus conclude that health discourse – and particularly the discourse of disease prevention – lends itself to analysis within the proximization framework. Moreover, it invites explorations in further public discourses using the rhetoric of threat and fear to force interventionist policies.

NOTE

1. Let alone intriguing metaphoric correspondences. Apart from the analogies listed by Van Rijn-van Tongeren (1997), note that (6) may force construal of the screening programs as intelligence, the infected *cells* as terrorist *cells*, the new treatment as air strikes *on* the terrorist cells, and the healthy cells as civilian population ('We now aim to..., doing minimal harm to healthy cells').

CHAPTER 4

Environmental Discourse: Climate Change

Abstract The focus of this chapter is on proximization strategies in today's environmental discourse, especially the discourse of climate change. It is claimed that threat construction in climate change discourse possesses a strategic character, constituting a prerequisite for legitimization of environmental policies. The strategies of proximization involve external physical threats, such as adverse weather phenomena, as well as internal threats, such as inaction, lack of environmental awareness and bad management. The chapter includes analyses of speeches by NATO leaders and the former California Governor Arnold Schwarzenegger.

Keywords Environmental discourse · Climate change · Green policies · Axiological proximization

Chapter 3 has shown that Proximization Theory (PT) provides a rich framework to study issues of fear and threat in health discourse. The aim of the present chapter is to analyse proximization strategies involved in threat construction in another important discourse of today, namely environmental discourse (Boykoff 2008; Berglez and Olausson 2010; Stibbe 2014; Bevitori 2014). In the following we focus on the discourse of climate change, where threat generation patterns occur most frequently. Similar to the health domain, threat construction in climate change discourse possesses a strategic character, constituting a prerequisite for legitimization of environmental policies. In climate change discourse, the construal of threat is nonetheless more complex, as the 'remote', 'other' entity – the ODC in technical terms – is not quite obvious and needs to be precisely defined. There is a direct 'external' impact, such as devastating natural phenomena which affect people, but also an indirect 'internal' impact, for instance, unsustainable environmental management. The discourse of climate change shows that the former is best construed by spatial and temporal proximization, while the latter often involves axiological proximization. The axiological element consists in the assignment of negative values to selected public actors, institutions and industry, situating them in the opposition to 'ordinary people', who are construed as the 'real self' entity.

CLIMATE CHANGE

Climate change is a relatively new domain of discourse studies, investigated mainly within the rapidly expanding CDA paradigm (Boykoff 2008; Berglez and Olausson 2010; Krzyżanowski 2009). Thus far, studies in climate change demonstrate a unilateral focus: most analyses concentrate on climate change as a form of transnational crisis. There are, however, two different ways in which this broad conception is approached in actual analysis. These different approaches result – probably – from two rather contradictory views that emerge from the media and the related discourses. On the one hand (Krzyżanowski 2009), there exists a tendency to frame climate change as a general issue of interest and critical importance to the entire societies and all social groups. Within that trend, climate change is described mainly as a threat to the entire humanity which thus must be dealt with by the entire societies or the global populace as a whole. On the other hand, the somewhat contradictory approach (Boykoff 2008) sees climate change as a problem which cannot be handled by the entire societies but by selected individuals who, due to their knowledge and expertise, are able to cope with different facets of climate change.

CLIMATE CHANGE AND PROXIMIZATION

Where does proximization, as an analytic device, belong, then? It seems that the former, 'global' view invites proximization better than the 'particularized' view. It would be quite unrealistic to count on the latter to help define the Self party and its agents in the first place. We have seen from the analysis of cancer discourse how difficult that might be. Considering that climate change is dealt with by a number of different (locationally, politically, rhetorically, perhaps also ideologically) individual expert voices in the vast and heterogeneous area of the global socio-political space, an attempt to ascribe any stable and homogeneous discursive strategies or practices to these actors would probably fail. However, if we focus on the global, institutionalized dimension of the discourse of climate change, the dimension that evens out the individual legitimization-rhetorical and other differences and conceptually consolidates the Self, chances emerge that proximization may indeed be applicable. To determine that applicability, and to demonstrate the role of proximization in threat and fear generation, we discuss excerpts from the speech 'Emerging Security Risks' by the NATO Secretary General Anders Fogh Rasmussen. The speech was given in London, on 1 October 2009:

(1) I want to devote a little more time today discussing the security aspects of climate change, because I think the time has come for a change in our approach.

First, I think we now know enough to start moving from analysis to action. Because the trend lines from climate change are clear enough, and grim enough, that we need to begin taking active steps to deal with this global threat.

We know that there will be more extreme weather events – catastrophic storms and flooding. If anyone doubts the security implications of that, look at what happened in New Orleans in 2006.

We know sea levels will rise. Two thirds of the world's population lives near coastlines. Critical infrastructure like ports, power plants and factories are all there. If people have to move they will do so in large numbers, always into where someone else lives, and sometimes across borders.

We know there will be more droughts. According to evidence, by 2025 about 40% of the world's population will be living in countries experiencing water shortages. Again, populations will have to move. And again, the security aspects could be devastating.

If you think I'm using dramatic language, let me draw your attention to one of the worst conflicts in the world, in Darfur. One of the main causes was a long drought. Both herders and farmers lost land, including to the desert. What happened? The nomads moved South, in search of grazing land – right to where the farmers are. Of course, a lot of other factors have contributed to what has happened – political decisions, religious differences and ethnic tensions. But climate change in Sudan has been a major contributor to this tragedy. And it will put pressure on peace in other areas as well. When it comes to climate change, the threat knows no borders.

There are more examples, but to my mind, the bottom line is clear. We may not yet know the precise effects, the exact costs or the definite dates of how climate change will affect security. But we already know enough to start taking action. This is my first point: either we start to pay now, or we will pay much more later.

You get the point. Climate change is different than any other threat we face today. The science is not yet perfect. The effects are just starting to be visible, and it's difficult to pin down what will actually change because of climate change. The timelines are not clear either. But that only makes the threat bigger. Sailors never thought the mythical North-West Passage would ever open. But it is opening. Anything's possible.

The security challenges being discussed today are big, and they are growing. They might also seem overwhelming. But I firmly believe that a lot can be done – to address the root causes, to minimize their impact, and to manage the effects when they hit.

Rasmussen's speech is an exemplary case of proximization rhetoric, bearing much similarity to the proximization discourse of anti-terrorism and military intervention. Except for the topic, it could well belong in the discourse of the Iraq war, which we have explored in Chap. 2. Rasmussen's construal of climate change is in terms of a global threat whose outlines are 'clear enough' and consequences 'devastating'; thus, an immediate action is necessary ('either we start to pay [costs of the climate change] now, or we will pay much more later'). Similar to the rhetoric of the Iraq war, the threat 'knows no borders' and a delay in response 'makes the threat bigger'. Analogy is used, like in the anti-terrorist discourse, to a past event (the war in Darfur), to endorse credibility of future visions. The visions involve construals of future events as personally consequential, thus strengthening the fear appeals ('Two thirds of the world's population lives near coastlines . . . If people have to move they will do so in large numbers, always into where someone else lives . . . '). Another familiar strategy is the construal of the moment of impact as virtually unpredictable ('the timelines are not clear'). Construing the climate change threat as continual and extending infinitely into the future, Rasmussen centralizes 'the now' and the near future as the most appropriate timeframe in which to act preventively.

At the micro level, Rasmussen's speech lends itself to analysis involving the canonical lexical markers of proximization, especially spatial proximization. Let us bring back (Table 4.1) the six lexico-grammatical categories of the spatial proximization framework we used in the study of the US anti-terrorist rhetoric in Chap. 2. Most phrases in Rasmussen's address match the items captured in the particular categories, 1 to 6. Note, for instance, the ample use of 'threat' (category 5), the use of 'catastrophic', 'tragedy' (category 6), or the presence of verbs in the progressive ('growing') marking the closeness of the threat (category 3). These spatial forms are strongly supported by temporal projections, which involve (i) the use of a modal auxiliary ('could') construing conditions increasing impact probability, and (ii) the application of the present perfect ('the time has come') construing change from the 'safe

Table 4.1 Spatial proximization framework and its key lexico-grammatical items (in anti-terrorist discourse, after Table 2.1)

Category	Key items
1. (NPs construed as elements of the deictic centre of the DS (IDCs))	['USA', 'United States', 'America']; ['American people', 'Americans', 'our people/nation/country/society']; ['free people/nations/countries/societies/world']; ['democratic people/nations/countries/societies/world']
2. (NPs construed as elements outside the deictic centre of the DS (ODCs))	['Iraq', 'Saddam Hussein', 'Saddam', 'Hussein']; ['Iraqi regime/dictatorship']; ['terrorists']; ['terrorist organizations/networks', 'Al-Qaeda']; ['extremists/radicals']; ['foreign regimes/dictatorships']
3. (VPs of motion and directionality construed as markers of movement of ODCs towards the deictic centre)	['are determined/intend to seek/acquire WMD']; ['might/may/could/can use WMD against *an IDC*]; ['expand/grow *in military capacity that could be directed against an IDC*]; ['move/are moving/head/are heading/have set their course toward confrontation *with an IDC*]
4. (VPs of action construed as markers of impact of ODCs upon IDCs)	['destroy *an IDC*]; ['set aflame/burn down *an IDC or IDC values*]
5. (NPs denoting abstract concepts construed as anticipations of impact of ODCs upon IDCs)	['threat']; ['danger']
6. (NPs denoting abstract concepts construed as effects of impact of ODCs upon IDCs)	['catastrophe']; ['tragedy']

past' to the 'threatening future'. The frequent repetitions of the 'will' phrases ('We know that there will be more extreme weather events') are a particularly noteworthy case. Resembling the 'typical' war on terror items captured in the third and the fourth category of the spatial framework, they have an even stronger appeal in Rasmussen's speech. This is due, first, to the epistemic modality marker ('will'), second, to the syntactic embedding of that marker, that is the entire evidential claim. At places, then, Rasmussen's climate change argument forces construals of threat in a more direct, appealing fashion than the 'canonical' or 'cradle' discourse of proximization, the anti-terrorist discourse.

Rasmussen's success in proximizing the climate change threat as an alert to action is not hindered by the global character of the threat. The globality of the threat does not result in vagueness or weakening of the ODC (i.e. the climate change) as an agent. Conversely, listing specific consequences such as storms, floodings, droughts, and linking them to specific places, regions or countries (New Orleans, Darfur, Sudan), concretizes the ODC in terms of its proven capacity to strike whichever part of the IDC's (i.e. the world) territory. This is obviously, as in any kind of interventionist discourse, the most effective prerequisite to solicit legitimization of preventive measures. The latter are missing from the speech but we can assume (which the later developments seem to prove) that the goal of Rasmussen's address is, first and foremost, to alert public attention to the gravity of the issue so the follow-up goals, involving specific actions, could be enacted as a matter of course. The spatial and temporal proximization strategies used in the speech make a significant contribution and, given the recurrence of some of the forms (for instance, all the lexical as well as grammatical forms construing the threat as growing with time), one can say that their application has been a strategic choice.

Catastrophic Visions and Ideological Oppositions

The discourse of climate change often links its apocalyptic projections to unmeasurable factors, such as unsustainable management, negligence, as well as ill will on the part of various public actors and industrial leaders, both institutional and individual. This involves attribution of negative values to the selected party or parties, which are thus construed as the ideological 'Other' standing in opposition to the 'Self', the 'ordinary people'. The construction of the ideological conflict (and its consequences) usually draws upon patterns of bipolar axiological representation and proximization. There are two major construals, both involving conceptual shifts. On the one hand, the adversarial posture of the Other (ODC) is shown as increasingly conducive to physical impact and destruction. On the other, the Self (IDC) is presented as mindful of certain historical events and analogies that underlie the present situation. These events and memories are recontextualized as background for the current judgment and decisions. The four excerpts below reveal both construals, embedded in larger patterns of policy legitimization. The excerpts come from four consecutive State of the State addresses (2007–2010) by the California Governor Arnold Schwarzenegger:

(2) There are some who don't see the threat. Some who pretend not to see it and some who don't want to see it. I think that global warming is real; it is a huge and growing problem. There is no single issue that is threatening the health and prosperity of our nation and humanity more than climate change.... The costs are high and they are growing. The cost of 19,000 people that are dying here in California alone every year because of smog, the cost of millions of hospital visits every year for smog related illnesses. I don't think that we can afford to waste any more time. (2007)
(3) We know what's going on with global warming and we know what's going on with the pollution, what kind of a health hazard it is. We must act because waiting only makes the threat bigger. We must act before the threat hits with its full force. California has taken the leadership role in fighting global warming and cleaning our environment, and we have worked very hard to pass laws in the last few years to make sure that we are fighting global warming and do everything to clean our environment. This is the challenge of our generation, and we will meet it with innovation and technology, and with total commitment that matches the greatest pioneers in our history, because that's the way California works. That's what California is all about. (2008)
(4) We can put not just our nation but the entire world on a path towards a clean and sustainable future. Wouldn't that be a great, great thing? Wouldn't that be a great legacy for our generation to do that? So this is why I say let's go to work, let's roll up our sleeves make it happen. 'There are some in the industry and over there in Washington DC who may not be on our side. But we have economics on our side. Since the supply of wind and sun and algae is unlimited, their prices will not jump. That cannot be said of oil, the supply of which is limited and declining. We are facing all of these challenges locally here, while in Washington they are still taking their time and they are not doing anything to act on curbing the greenhouse gas emissions. (2009)

(5) It used to be that we could sit and wait. But the last years have changed all that. The time has come to start adopting green policies as fast as we can develop them, because this is the only way to go and that's how we can inspire the creation of new technology, which will save us all. Some have argued that we can still wait and that's an option. In my view, it's the riskiest of all options. Being dependent on one source of fuel leaves our economy and our national security vulnerable to price shocks and global events beyond our control. Hydrogen [as a fuel source in cars] leaves no trail of pollution and causes no global warming. Using it does not fund the terrorists who would destroy us. (2010)

The common function of texts (2), (3), (4) and (5) is to construct a legitimization frame for a continual implementation of clean energy policies, providing an effective yet very costly alternative to toxic gas emissions. Under the Assembly Bill (AB) 32, or the 'California Global Warming Solutions Act of 2006', California will reduce its greenhouse gas emissions to 1990 levels by 2020, which roughly equates to a 15 % reduction. In 2011 the California Air Resources Board adopted a cap-and-trade program, which covers the 'major sources of [greenhouse gas] emissions in the State such as refineries, power plants, industrial facilities and transportation fuels' (Air Resources Board 2013). The program commenced in 2012, and 'enforceable compliance obligations' came into effect in relation to emissions generated in 2013. It is planned that the cap-and trade program will aid the achievement of an 80 % reduction of emissions, as dictated by AB 32. The Low Carbon Fuel Standard, which was issued in 2007, 'calls for a reduction of at least 10 % in the carbon intensity of California's transportation fuels by 2020'. Overall, it is estimated that these regulations will result in an '18 % reduction in climate change emissions from the light-duty fleet [of vehicles] in 2020 and a 27 % reduction in 2030.' (Air Resources Board 2014). Further investments include the Million Solar Roof Initiative, which offers tax incentives to the general public in return for installing solar panels on their homes; and the Hydrogen Highway project, which is designed to ensure that those who buy hydrogen powered cars will have access to hydrogen fuelling stations throughout the state. Altogether, the cost of green energy solutions adopted in the state of California in the years 2005–2015 is estimated at $2.4 billion, a truly staggering amount. To legitimize this size of investment, Governor Schwarzenegger develops a complex rhetorical stance, in which threat and fear generation patterns are skilfully complemented by ideological appeals.

First and foremost, the calibre of the environmental threat is considered in relation to the attitudes and social postures of those responsible for containing it. The threat is depicted as 'huge', 'growing' and ultimately devastating unless there is a reaction ((3) 'We must act because waiting only makes the threat bigger. We must act before the threat hits with its full force'). The gravity of the moment is construed through temporal proximization of an emerging danger. The 'before' phrase presupposes an external impact, yet without specifying when it might actually occur. This adds to the threat at the conceptual level, since there is no clue when to react. At the lexical level, the word 'threat' produces a similar effect. As a nominalization, 'threat' conflates the present and the future; it represents an objectified entity that exists at the present moment and presages an ominous future. It thus creates an intriguing effect of 'continual momentousness': the threat can materialize anytime. These scary visions are set against the background of mutually opposite opinions, ideas and attitudes of people and institutions which are supposed to handle the crisis situation. On the one hand, the California government and its people are presented as rational, resourceful and positively inspired by their state legacy ((3) 'This is the challenge of our generation, and we will meet it with innovation and technology, and with total commitment that matches the greatest pioneers in our history, because that's the way California works. That's what California is all about'). On the other, the 'adversaries' (the federal government and, most probably, the nationally owned and/or controlled companies) are described as passive, incompetent or plainly cunning and cynical ((2) 'There are some who don't see the threat. Some who pretend not to see it and some who don't want to see it'; (4) 'There are some in the industry and over there in Washington DC who may not be on our side'). The legitimization of the state policies is thus built on the positive image of the 'Self' group (the State and its people), as well as the negative image of the 'Other' group (the central government and part of the state industry). The negative conceptualization of the Other is particularly appealing and legitimization-effective, as their inaction and ill will make the threat grow quickly enough to warrant prompt response from the local government. The proximization of the threat involves thus both the spatio-temporal construal of imminence of the greenhouse effect, and the multiplication of the contributing socio-political and ideological factors.

The construction of the ideological conflict in (2–5) rests on a 'competition' between two political postures (active and committed vs. passive and negligent) which determine two disparate scenarios construed as parallel extensions of the present. The scenarios develop in a quasi-dialogic discourse stretch, in which Governor Schwarzenegger presents two conflicting views of the future, one of which can be described as 'privileged' and the other as 'oppositional' (Dunmire 2011). The privileged future (the growth of the greenhouse threat) is a future that is highly probable and thus requiring a response Schwarzenegger favours over an alternative response (or a lack thereof). The oppositional future presupposes a 'we can sit and wait' view, which holds that there is no imminent threat and, consequently, no preventive steps are necessary. This view is presented as contradictory to evidence ('The cost of 19,000 people that are dying here in California alone every year because of smog, the cost of millions of hospital visits every year for smog related illnesses') and is contrasted with the privileged view, which is conceptualized as informed, knowledge-based and rational. The rationality of the privileged view consists in a thorough consideration of the past state of affairs and its comparison with the present state. One of the key strategies Schwarzenegger engages to draw such a comparison is a contrastive use of grammatical tenses: the simple past ('It used to be that we could sit and wait') and the present perfect ('But the last years have changed all that. The time has come to start adopting green policies...'). The contrastive pattern marks a clean break from the safe past and, above all, a predefined, continually threatening future extending *infinitely* from that past.

Lastly, it is easy to notice that almost any time a strong fear appeal is made based on spatio-temporal proximization of the Other, a balancing positive appeal is delivered, involving axiological proximization of the central values of the Self. This can be seen in (3) ('California has taken the leadership role. This is the challenge of our generation, and we will meet it with innovation and technology, and with total commitment that matches the greatest pioneers in our history, because that's the way California works'), as well as (4) ('We can put not just our nation but the entire world on a path towards a clean and sustainable future. Wouldn't that be a great, great thing? Wouldn't that be a great legacy for our generation to do that? So this is why I say let's go to work, let's roll up our sleeves make it happen'). The strategic interplay of the two distinct appeals reflects the logic of the thesis-antithesis formula as described and advocated by the Rhetorical Structure Theory (Mann and Thompson 1988).

The RST holds that for best argumentative effects, the speaker's positive claim (the thesis part) should follow the opening negative claim (the antithesis). That way, the positive claim is better remembered and can serve to legitimize direct action. Governor Schwarzenegger's speeches contain several examples of the RST formula, for instance, (3) starts with issues of public concern, such as pollution and health hazards, which subsequently give way to a reassuring ideological call. Interestingly, the call draws upon another pragma-rhetorical strategy, which can be described as 'complimenting the hearer' (Brown and Levinson 1987, among others). By paying compliments (to the hearer and/or the hearer and himself), the speaker expresses appreciation and solidarity between the parties and enacts mental 'common ground' as a prerequisite for soliciting involvement of the hearer in a joint course of action. In Schwarzenegger's speech of 2008 (3), the strategy of complimenting is particularly appealing and credible, as it builds on past facts ('California has taken the leadership role in fighting global warming and cleaning our environment, and we have worked very hard to pass laws in the last few years to make sure that we are fighting global warming and do everything to clean our environment'). It thus abides by the core rule of *consistency*, which we discussed in Chap. 1.

The Controversial 'Other' and Axiological Proximization

The smooth interplay of the spatio-temporal and axiological proximization strategies in texts such as Rasmussen's and Schwarzenegger's warrants the applicability of proximization and PT to studies in climate change discourse. It seems that PT is particularly well suited to elucidate the twofold nature of climate change rhetoric, which involves the presence of fear appeals and threat generation patterns, as well as calls to ideological awareness, pride and civic legacy. At the same time, climate change discourse informs PT with regard to two central elements of the STA proximization model. First, similar to health discourse, it provides a fine-grained insight into the complex status of the conceptual 'Other'. The Other in climate change texts cannot be accounted for unless recognized with respect to a physical or abstract ODC category, such as weather phenomena, climate policies or institutions managing climate change. Each of these distinct categories makes for a different proximization arrangement and thus a different proximization strategy. While the impact of natural phenomena can be perceived as physical and tangible, the 'impact' of environmental inaction is in comparison intangible – though it is, somewhat paradoxically, equally cumulative. The number of potential ODCs in climate change discourse seems high and probably higher than in health discourse, let alone state political discourse, the original domain of proximization. We thus need to exercise an increasingly greater caution when it comes to the conceptual groundwork for textual analysis. The other important insight that climate change data offer is the extra focus on axiological proximization. Whereas the 'standard' construal of axiological proximization involves the piling up of adversarial negative values, climate change discourse relies at least to the same extent upon the 'positive' proximization of home values, which are conceptualized as elements of historical legacy triggering public mobilization. That said, climate change texts emerge as venues of deeply ideological struggle, where the presence or absence of a given set of values is directly linked to a specific social behaviour.

CHAPTER 5

Technological Discourse: Threats in the Cyberspace

Abstract This chapter demonstrates that the original terrain of Proximization Theory, anti-terrorist discourse, has expanded to blend with other domains, such as discourse of cyberspace. Originally a mundane technological discourse, the discourse of cyberspace has changed drama-tically after 9/11, incorporating fear-inducing alerts to the possibility of cyberattacks. The chapter shows that, today, the discourse of cyberspace has virtually turned into the discourse of cyberthreat, reflecting general context of uncertainty and common anxiety following the WTC and the Pentagon terrorist attacks. It includes a variety of proximization strategies which construe 'clear and present' threats in order to trigger public mobilization and response.

Keywords Cyberspace · Cyber-terrorist discourse · Cyber-fear · Electronic Pearl Harbor

The term 'technological discourse' can be interpreted in two ways; first, as a jargon used to exchange in-field specialized information, second, as a public discourse concerned with technological progress and its conse-quences. The discussion in this chapter draws, obviously, on the second interpretation. Specifically, we focus on the rapid technological advance-ment as an urgent security issue, growing in its importance in the last couple of years. The seriousness of this issue reflects in an ever-increasing

P. Cap, *The Language of Fear*, DOI 10.1057/978-1-137-59731-1_5

53

number of publications, such as books, articles as well as media reports, alerting the public to various hazards and threats that modern technology can create unless powerful control means are promptly put in place. Particular concern is over the power of information technologies as, potentially, mighty weapons in the hands of terrorists to launch cyberattacks on public digital networks. The loud voices demanding steps to prevent such catastrophic events from happening constitute a specific discourse, which furthers its goals through fear appeals and other forms of discursive coercion. It is thus an essentially legitimization discourse, even though the producers of particular texts are not necessarily state leaders, but most of the time individuals (scientists, journalists, media experts, etc.) acting 'on behalf' of the general public (Sandwell 2006; Graham 2004). While not possessing directly executive powers, they aim to describe the threat and pre-legitimize preventive actions which they propose to policymakers. Their fear-based, hard-hitting rhetoric lends itself, with a number of reservations, to proximization analysis. This shows, from a methodological standpoint, that Proximization Theory (PT) may be applicable well beyond the state-controlled discourse.

THE DISCOURSE OF CYBER-TERROR

According to Sandwell (2006), the discourse of cyber-terror is a direct consequence of 9/11; cyberthreats are construed within the 'general context of uncertainty and common anxiety' following the WTC and the Pentagon terrorist attacks (Sandwell 2006, p. 11). The most extreme manifestations of cyber-fear, says Sandwell, are articulated around the 'post-9/11 boundary dissolving threats, intrusive alterities, and existential ambivalences created by the erosion of binary distinctions and hierarchies that are assumed to be constitutive principles of everyday life' (Sandwell 2006, p. 40). As such, the discourse of cyber-terror is not merely a US discourse, it is a world discourse. Its principal practitioners are the world media, media experts, and the press in particular, which, on Sandwell's view, perpetuate the threat by creating mixed representations of 'the off-line and the online world, the real or physical and the virtual or imagined' (Sandwell 2006, p. 40).

Neither Sandwell (2006) nor other scholars (e.g. Graham 2004) are precise about the motives that underlie such fear-inducing representations. This is unfortunate since establishing the motives is of clear relevance to the analysis of the discourse of cyber-terror as a legitimization discourse.

There are however two hypotheses that emerge from data analysis. On the first, the media discourse of cyber-terror has a strong political purpose: it aims to alert the people, the government and state's security structures to the seriousness of the issue, thus exerting pressure on the state to implement or strengthen defense measures. Such a discourse can be considered a legitimization discourse since the measures become pre-legitimized by discourse construals reflecting a true intent to influence the state's policies. On the other hypothesis, the press representations of cyber-terror have, instead of or apart from political motives, a strong commercial purpose and one of the central aims is to increase readership.

The data evidence to determine the ultimate correctness of the hypotheses is limited. Thus, in the proximization analysis that follows we cannot help speculations at the coercion-legitimization level. In other words, we cannot tell with an absolute certainty *why* the proximization strategies, *as a whole*, have been used. Still, it is thought-provoking to see so many of different proximization forms operate within just two relatively small texts. The texts are excerpts from a book by Dan Verton, a respected IT journalist working with the influential *Computerworld* magazine.[1] In the book (2003), he recaps the thoughts presented in the 2002 issues of the *Computerworld*:

(1) This is the emerging face of the new terrorism. It is a thinking man's game that applies the violent tactics of the old world to the realities and vulnerabilities of the new high-tech world. Gone are the days when the only victims are those who are unfortunate enough to be standing within striking distance of the blast. Terrorism is now about smart, well-planned indirect targeting of the electronic sinews of the whole nations. Terrorists are growing in their evil capacity to turn our greatest technologies against us. Imagine, one day, overloaded digital networks, resulting in the collapse of finance and e-commerce networks, collapsed power grids and non-functioning telephone networks. Imagine, another day, the collapse, within seconds, of air traffic control systems, resulting in multiple airplane crashes; or of any other control systems, resulting in widespread car and train crashes, and nuclear meltdowns. Meanwhile, the perpetrators of the war remain undetected behind their distant, encrypted terminals, free to bring the world's mightiest nations to their knees with a few keystrokes in total impunity. (Verton 2003, p. 55)
(2) Armed with nothing but a laptop and a high speed Internet connection, a computer geek could release a fast spreading computer virus that in a matter of minutes gives him control of thousands, perhaps millions, of personal computers and servers throughout the world. This drone

army launches a silent and sustained attack on computers that are crucial for sending around the billions of packets of data that keep e-mail, the Web and other, more basic necessities of modern life humming. At first the attack seems to be an inconvenience – e-mail traffic grinds to a halt, Web browsing is impossible. But then the problems spread to services only tangentially related to the Internet: your automated-teller machine freezes up, your emergency call fails to get routed to police stations and ambulance services, airport- and train-reservation systems come down. After a few hours, the slowdown starts to affect critical systems: the computers that help run power grids, air-traffic control and telephone networks. (Verton 2003, p. 87)

Analysis

Similar to the discourse of climate change, (1) and (2) include a number of fearful anticipations and alerts to the imminence of a gathering threat. To make the threat global, they construe a broad spectrum of the IDC entities: it seems from the texts that there is no entity in the world, whether a nation or an individual, that is *not* under threat. This construal involves several lexico-grammatical ploys, such as, in (1), the abundant pluralization of the affected entities (e.g., 'victims', 'nations', 'networks', 'systems') or, in (2), depicting the cyberthreat in personally consequential terms (*'your* automated-teller machine freezes up, *your* emergency call fails to get routed to police stations and ambulance services'). Analytically, the texts reiterate the problem with demarcating the ODC entities. Unless we take Verton's 'cyber-terrorists' as 'terrorists' in the ideological, geopolitical and locational sense of alterity that we have recognized so far, we have to approach them as, in a way, isolated 'ODC cells' among the IDC entities. This dilemma may well be unresolvable given the short history of the cyberthreat discourse and the resulting shortage of data, especially reference data. Thus, the part of the conceptual scenario that remains most in line with the 'default' proximization scenario is the act of proximization as such, the symbolic shift of the threatening entity in the direction of the IDC entities. Though neither (1) nor (2) give a clear picture of the *source* of the threat, they include a large number of lexico-grammatical forms construing its speed, imminence, as well as devastating effects.

Most of these forms echo the language choices and strategies from, again, the war on terror discourse. They also reveal – to the benefit of Proximization as a theory – several features of the discourses that have been studied in Chaps. 3 and 4. The cyberthreat is construed as redefining, once and for all, the 'old world' security arrangement ([1]: 'Gone are the days when...'). The 'new world' arrangement is far more 'vulnerable': not only are the 'old' ideologies of 'evil' and 'violence' still in existence, they are now 'exercised' with new and formidable ('high-tech') tools. As a result, the threat is 'growing', its 'blast' could now reach the entire 'nations', and the impact is virtually unpredictable: it may come 'one day' or 'another'. Both (1) and (2) construe the impact as ultra-fast ([1]: 'within seconds'; [2]: 'fast spreading', 'in a matter of minutes') and massively destructive ([1]: 'airplane crashes', 'nuclear meltdowns'; [2]: 'affect critical systems'). All the lexical forms which force such an ominous conceptualization are apparently categorizable in terms of the 'spatial', 'temporal' and 'axiological' items of proximization as recognized by PT. For instance, the 'fast spreading' phrase performs spatial and temporal proximization, the 'blast' performs spatial proximization, and 'one day' enacts indefiniteness and thus uncertainty about the future, in line with the strategy of temporal proximization. In contrast to health discourse, as well as the majority of environmental discourse, there are also phrases which force axiological construals ('evil capacity', 'violent tactics'). Intriguingly, text (2) includes a discourse sequence that resembles President Bush's argument linking the ideologies of 'dictatorship and radicalism' to the later material impact ('brings danger to our own people' – recall the analysis in Chap. 2). The sequence in question leads from 'At first the attack seems to be an inconvenience' to 'After a few hours, the slowdown starts to affect critical systems'. Though it includes no ideological element, it still forces a conceptualization whereby an initially minor glitch turns over time into a real, 'tangible' threat.

REASONING BY ANALOGY

Drawing on fears instilled in the public space by the 9/11 attacks, the discourse of cyber-terror makes ample use of historical flashbacks and analogies, whose function is to endorse credibility of future visions by linking them to real events of the past. Catastrophic past events are thus proximized and conflated with current developments. As a result, the current events, as well as projections, increase their dramatic appeal. The main reference point is, naturally, the 9/11 itself, but there are other and more distant analogies too, such as 'electronic Pearl Harbor' and

'Waterloo'. The accuracy of some of these analogies is disputable, revealing the manipulative potential of cyber-terror discourse.

Electronic Pearl Harbor

Winn Schwartau of infowar.com first used the term 'Electronic Pearl Harbor' in testimony before the US Congress as early as 1991 (Schwartau 1994, p. 43). This analogy links the cyber security debate to a 'real' and successful surprise attack on critical US military infrastructures during World War II while, simultaneously, warning against the idea of American invulnerability due to its geographical position. The Pearl Harbor analogy is used with startling frequency in the US and world media as a shorthand description of the likely consequences of a cyber-terrorist attack on the US. A Lexis-Nexis search of major world newspapers finds 205 mentions of this and related terms in the twenty years between 1994 and 2014.

Another play on words that has found favour in the media is the term 'electronic Waterloo'. Its 1994–2014 frequency is however considerably smaller: a LexisNexis search reveals (only) 85 mentions of the term. Such a big difference begs several questions, as it has been asserted that the Waterloo analogy is the more accurate of the two. The visions conjured up by reference to an 'electronic Pearl Harbor' are of a sudden crippling blow against critical infrastructures resulting in panic, chaos and destruction. However, it has been argued that this 'bolt-out-of-the-blue scenario' is not the most significant cyberwarfare threat to America. The greater danger, according to analysts at the US Center for Strategic and International Studies, is a meticulously planned, carefully executed campaign by a focused adversary with a thorough grounding in information warfare techniques. The most important feature of such a strategy, according to the CSIS 2014 report, would be its contribution to important strategic goals as part of a larger-scale, possibly long-term strategy. It would not, in other words, be intended simply to gain the public spotlight, create havoc or win a temporary edge in battle:

> Although the attack on Pearl Harbor precipitated major strategic change, the attack itself was a single blow that failed to achieve Japan's strategic objective, which was to force the US to an accommodation more favorable to Japan's then expansive foreign policy. The more significant information warfare threat would likely resemble not Pearl Harbor but instead Waterloo,

where technology, planning, and careful execution were used as part of a long-range plan aimed at altering the world's political, military and economic order. (CSIS 2014: 2)

The prevalence of an 'electronic Pearl Harbor' over 'electronic Waterloo' in the US and world media shows, apparently, the necessity for the proximized threat images and related analogies to have immediate resonance and attract wide understanding. The aim of such a discourse is not actually to be informative or explanatory, but to manufacture fear and to do so in the simplest and most direct way possible.

Weapons of Mass Disruption

In the wake of 9/11, threats to the integrity of US information infrastructure have been ascribed a level of urgency analogous to nuclear and biological threats, which has galvanized the relationship between IT and security as a primary policy consideration in the US (Yould 2003, p. 75). In September 2002, Richard Clarke, former Special White House Advisor for Cyberspace Security, told ABC News: 'Cyberterrorism is easier to do than building a weapon of mass destruction. Cyberattacks *are* a weapon of mass disruption, and they're a lot cheaper and easier' (Wallace 2002). Howard Schmidt, Clarke's one-time deputy, has also repeatedly referred to the threat from 'weapons of mass disruption' (McGray 2003). But even before 9/11 the American 'cyber-angst' was palpable (Bendrath 2003). As early as 1999, Congressman Curt Weldon (R-Pennsylvania) placed cyberterrorism at the top of his list of modern threats to the American way of life. Speaking at the 1999 InfoWarCon conference to an audience of uniformed military personnel, corporate IT managers, computer security consultants and at least one screenwriter, Weldon said: 'In my opinion, neither missile proliferation nor weapons of mass destruction are as serious as the threat of cyberterrorism'. In May 2001, Senator Robert Bennett (R-Utah), stated: 'Attacks against the US banking system would devastate the United States more than a nuclear device let off over a major city' (Porteus 2001). At around the same time, Michael Specter (2001), author of The New Yorker article alluded to above, predicting: 'The Internet is waiting for its Chernobyl, and I don't think we will be waiting much longer'. Such predictions are not limited to US commentators. A 2003 Newsweek article quoted John Naughton, described as 'an Internet expert at Britain's Open University', as saying 'If I were Al Qaeda, I wouldn't waste time with nuclear weapons. I'd be going to Microsoft training courses' (Adams and Guterl 2003). In her seminal article on the role of linguistic metaphors, puns and acronyms in the field of nuclear defense strategy, Cohn (1987) demonstrates how specific uses of language are used to dedramatize the actual, growing threat. It seems that, with regard to the cyber-terrorist threat, exactly the opposite is happening. Far from derealizing the threat, much of the discourse of cyberterrorism mobilized by the media fosters the formulation of vociferous phrases and fearful buzzwords. The example is John Naughton's ultimate designation of cyberthreats as 'weapons of mass disruption' (Adams and Guterl 2003), which is directly analogous to 'weapons of mass destruction', that is nuclear, biological or chemical weapons. Since its coinage in 2003, the phrase has appeared multiple times in both the US and world press (Jarvis 2016).

While hugely popular and appealing as a fear-generating device, the phrase 'weapons of mass disruption' seems essentially inaccurate and unhelpful in terms of advancing ideas about the relationship between national security and IT. This is true whether one believes such threats are imminent or one is sceptical of the cyber-terrorist threat. For sceptics, for example, equating the effects of a cyberattack on the US banking system with the effects of the Chernobyl disaster is not only an exaggeration that defies corroboration, but is extremely disingenuous suggesting as it does that the physical (and continuing) death of not just large numbers of people, but literally the whole of a vast territory, is less significant than its digital disconnection. The functions of such comparisons are clear however: 'Urgency; state power claiming the legitimate use of extraordinary means. . . . Survival might sound overly dramatic but it is, in fact, the survival of the unit as a basic political unit – a sovereign state – that is the key' (Jarvis 2016, p. 10). Public perceptions are thus messaged, so that urgent issues such as cyberterrorism, portrayed as having this 'undercutting' potential are accepted as having to be addressed prior to all others because, if they are not, the state will cease to exist as a sovereign entity, and all other questions will thus be irrelevant. This is, rhetorically, in line with the principle of consistency, which we have discussed in Chap. 1.

IDENTIFYING ANTAGONISTIC ACTORS

The discursive securitization of cyberterrorism involves defining the specific hostile actors. This has never been easy, posing a challenge for analysis of particular texts in terms of PT. Traditionally, the focus in security policy analysis has been on potentially threatening states or governments, but in debates about terrorism and information warfare it has been emphasized that non-state actors too may pose a threat. The idea that anonymous adversaries might attempt to penetrate information systems from virtually anywhere in the world breaks with the traditional understanding of security – that the identity, location and goals of the enemy are known – and increases the sense of fear and insecurity. Eriksson (2001) argues that 'the introduction of non-state enemies in security thinking implies opening up Pandora's box, as the number of potential enemies in "cyberspace" is virtually unlimited' (Eriksson 2001, p. 218). In terms of IT security, Sandwell (2006) posits five different types of antagonistic actors: insiders, hackers, criminals, corporations, governments and terrorists. Conceptually and analytically, each of these 'ODC' groups reveals a different positioning in discourse space (DS). The patterns of discursive coercion involving proximization of an external threat are thus also different – though interrelated – as these examples demonstrate (italics added):

(3) The so-called *hacker intrusions* not only cost Defense tens of millions of dollars, but pose a serious threat to our national security. Without increased attention by Defense top management and continued oversight by the Congress, security weaknesses will continue. *Hackers and our adversaries* will keep compromising sensitive Defense systems.

(4) Air Force officials at Wright-Patterson Air Force Base told us that, on average, they receive 3,000 to 4,000 attempts to access information each month from countries all around the world. It is quite possible that at least one of the *hackers* may have been working for a *foreign country* interested in obtaining military research data or learning what the Air Force is working on.

(5) We do have evidence that computer-related education and training courses conducted by *nation-state sponsored organizations* are being attended by those who go on to act *independently*. Some of us have strong suspicions that there is occasionally some foreknowledge by *those actually conducting the training* that that is why the training was being pursued by *certain individuals*.

(6) Because of the seriousness and gravity of the potential consequences, we never discount and remain very vigilant to, the possibility of foreign intelligence exploitation by *nation-states* whom we know have the capability to conduct cyber-terrorist activities.

All the examples come from an interview with Jack L. Brock, Director of US Defense Information and Financial Management Systems. The interview took place on CNN on 2 May 2006, three days before a

Congressional debate on possible increase in federal funding for IT security agencies. In an attempt to rationalize the needs of his agency, Brock paints a complex picture of the ominous cyberthreat, involving multiple agents and antagonistic groups. The hostile actors differ in specificity: while the activity of hackers (3, 4) is presented in terms of concrete evil acts ('intrusions'), the activity of hostile states (4, 5, 6) is not immediately obvious and visible; it consists in harbouring, supporting or merely tolerating the organizations and individuals that pose a cyber-terrorist threat. There are thus, despite individual differences, some clear links between the antagonistic entities, creating a complex impact network. This is where the discourse of cyberterrorism borrows, again, from the discourse of state terrorism in general. We have observed in Chap. 2 that the American (anti-)terrorist rhetoric often combines direct fear appeals with ideological descriptions of the enemy entity. The function of these descriptions is to present the antagonistic mind-sets or values as triggers for invasive actions (Fig. 5.1). We can see from Jack L. Brock's interview that in the discourse of cyberterrorism foreign state adversaries are frequently construed as ideological cradles of cyber-terrorist actions, such as hacking or virus-spreading. The destructive consequences of these actions are depicted as last in a cause-and-effect chain, which takes the space of a single sentence (as in [6]), or several sentences (as in [3]-[4]-[5]). Since the connection between 'the ideological' and 'the actual/physical' is implicit in the chain, description of the proximized impact is not confined to the final syntactic or textual position; in fact, it often occurs at the very beginning of the chain (as for instance in [6]), for emphasis and appeal.

Manipulation and Abuse

The Self–Other arrangement in Fig. 5.1 reflects the deeply manipulative potential of cyber-terrorist discourse. As can be imagined, the extension of the Other (ODC) category to include several types of outside agents, such as foreign states, institutions, as well as individuals performing the actual cyberattacks, easily blurs the boundaries of criminal or terrorist activities and potentially justified online activism. This conflation has quickly gone beyond the level of discourse. In an admittedly simplified approach, most computer intrusions in the US are now classifiable under terrorism (Jarvis 2016). In legislation, the mere suspicion of terrorism gives the authorities disproportionate rights, such as extended periods of custody without filing

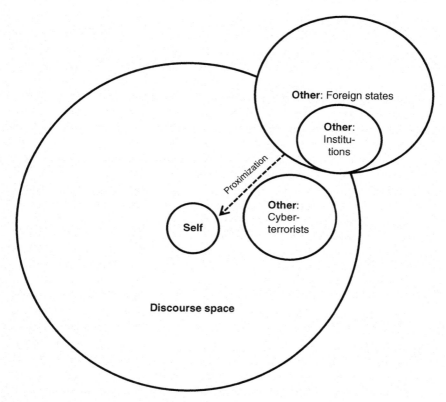

Fig. 5.1 Proximization in cyber-terrorist discourse

actual charges, or the possibility of capital punishment if convicted. The executive branch, in turn, has the right to undertake the entire process from accusation to punishment outside the public eye in protected and secret military tribunals. One undoubted implication of these regulations on online political activism is that if the state reacts to terrorism as war, any act of disruptive or destructive activism in the cyberspace falls potentially into the category of cyberterrorism, or even cyberwar.

The sensitivity of cyber-terrorist discourse to political manipulation and abuse has provoked a number of voices in academia. In an important contribution to the debate on the importance of terminological clarity regarding cyberterrorism and online political activism, Vegh (2012) examines the potential of cyberterrorism and provides a possible model to prepare for 'information warfare.' He clarifies the terminological ambiguities of terrorism and crime, as applied to cyberspace, and points out the necessarily different legislative, law enforcement and national security responses. Vegh declares that 'labeling every malicious use of computer systems as "terrorism" serves only to exacerbate confusion and even panic among users and the general public, and frequently hinders prosecution and prevention by blurring the motivations behind the crime' (Vegh 2012, p. 36). Therefore, it is imperative to underline that terminological ambiguities, sanctioned by discourse practice, do have serious policy and legislative implications. The interrogation of language used by official sources and print news media is, argues Vegh, of utmost importance.

It seems that the print media in the US are indeed in need of a thorough terminological revision. Since 2001, there have been multiple cases of using terms such as 'hackers', 'terrorists', 'cyber-terrorists', 'cyber-attackers', 'cyber-criminals', etc., interchangeably and indiscriminately, with respect to all acts as well as anticipations of computer intrusions. As a result, journalists have been able to provide their stories with increasingly longer lists of possible terrorist targets. In a recent article asserting that the US government is now prepared to respond militarily to any cyberattack, the author enumerates: 'Hackers, criminals and terrorists could gain access to the digital controls for the nation's main utilities, power grids, air traffic control systems and nuclear power plants' (Gellman 2012). He goes on to find evidence to a potential cyberattack in the planning: 'Routed through telecommunications switches in Saudi Arabia, Indonesia and Pakistan, the visitors who cased Bay Area computers studied emergency telephone systems, electrical generation and transmissions, water storage and distribution, nuclear power plants and gas facilities' (Gellman 2012). Most of these scenarios are derived from a 2001 seminal article by Barry Collin titled 'The Future of Cyberterrorism' (Collin 2001) and his claims about the apparent vulnerability of the US computer-controlled systems (from air traffic control systems to cereal production lines). Collin's article describes various acts of online intrusion, naming the perpetrators interchangeably as 'attackers', 'hackers' and 'criminals'. The article ends with the assertion that, in actuality, all these intrusion acts are 'terrorist acts', which must be stopped with 'strong anti-terrorist measures'. Apart from blurring the boundaries between different kinds of online intrusion, the article prescribes another lexical convention. It contains an unprecedented number of modality markers which conflate the present and the future into one temporal frame characterized by the continuing presence of an outside threat. The main marker used in the text is, as exemplified above, the verb *could*, which construes a grave and ominous threat existing in the present and extending infinitely into the future. The threat is thus proximized through its indefiniteness: there is no clue when to expect the impact.

Discourse of Cyberspace versus Discourses of Health and Environment

Compared to health discourse and environmental discourse, the discourse of cybersspace reveals, technically, a similar DS arrangement. First, it broadens the conceptual 'Self' camp to include as many IDC agents (people, governments, economies, computer-controlled systems) as possible. Thereby, it extends the landscape of threat over a vast territory of home entities, prompting them to react. Second, it amplifies the threat by making it at the same time conspicuous and indefinite. On the one hand, there are plentiful adversaries (hostile governments, institutions, individuals) and thus plentiful sources of the potential impact. On the other, none of these adversary groups is specific enough to constitute, as has been said, a threat of clear temporal outlines. This is where the discourse of cyberspace and cyberterrorism meets directly with the discourse of climate change: both of them draw upon people's inner fears and threatening speculations.

There are however some differences as well. Compared to health discourse and, especially, environmental discourse, the discourse of cyberspace contains practically no axiological element. Unlike the rhetoric of climate change, for instance, it does not prescribe clear links between postures and actions of the antagonistic groups; nor does it link its fearful anticipations to the negligence and inaction on the part of the home group. It seems that the external impact construed in the discourse of cyberspace and cyberterrorism is so extensive and appealing that it needs no further warrant, except analogy. Indeed, conceptual analogies and historical flashbacks are frequent in cyber-terrorist rhetoric, establishing a connection between cyber-terrorist actions and 'real-terrorist' acts, such as 9/11. The number of analogies in cyber-terrorist discourse is in fact significantly higher than in health and environmental discourses. This makes cyber-terrorist rhetoric rely on predominantly spatial and temporal strategies of proximization, which serve to construe the past events as premises for the current and future actions.

NOTE

1. www.computerworld.com

CHAPTER 6

Immigration and Anti-migration Discourses: The Early Rhetoric of Brexit

Abstract The focus of this last chapter is on immigration, a theme that has been salient in public discourse of the modern UK, especially the 'Brexit' rhetoric, where it encroached on issues of national sovereignty, democracy and economic prosperity. The chapter shows that the British immigration discourse is to a large extent a discourse of uncertainty and ever-growing anxiety, as well as xenophobia and hatred, involving a strong Self–Other distinction and organized ways of othering. It relies on discursively constructed threat and fear generation mechanisms, such as proximization, which perform a coercive function. The chapter analyses data from state political and media discourses, including speeches by David Cameron and Nigel Farage, as well as newspaper editorials and commentaries.

Keywords Immigration · Anti-migration discourse · Brexit · UK referendum debate

This last chapter is being written shortly after a momentous event in the history of the modern Europe: the UK's referendum on EU membership. On 23 June 2016, after a long and heated campaign, 52 % of the British people cast their votes in favour of leaving the Union. Voting for 'Brexit', they put an end to the 24-year long period of UK's membership in the EU as one of its founding states. The promise to hold the referendum was first announced by the British PM David Cameron in January 2013, subject to

© The Author(s) 2017
P. Cap, *The Language of Fear*, DOI 10.1057/978-1-137-59731-1_6

the condition that the Conservative party win the next general election in 2015. The year 2013 was thus the first year of the 'proto-referendum' debate, defining the main themes, attitudes, ideological positions and their representations in public discourse for the following three years. In this chapter we focus on immigration, a theme that has been particularly salient in UK's discourse of 2013, encroaching on several other issues such as national sovereignty, democracy and economic prosperity. As will be shown, the immigration discourse in 2013 Britain is to a large extent the discourse of uncertainty and ever-growing anxiety, as well as xenophobia and hatred, involving a strong Self–Other distinction and organized ways of othering. Much of this discourse is characterized by linguistic operations that draw upon spatial cognition and construed movement, such as proximization. We support these claims by examining the following data:

- Prime Minister David Cameron's speech at Bloomberg on 23 January 2013. As noted by Todd (2015), this speech sets the terms for the debate over the rest of the year and virtually the entire period preceding the referendum;
- Parliamentary debates on the European Union (Referendum) Bill 2013. This Bill stipulated that a referendum on the UK's membership of the EU must be held before the end of 2017. The Bill was not introduced by the government because the Liberal Democrats (currently in coalition with the larger Conservative Party) did not agree with Cameron's referendum commitment. Instead, a Conservative backbencher introduced the legislation as a Private Member's Bill.[1] The Bill completed its passage through the House of Commons on 29 November 2013, but failed to make it through the House of Lords. While a Private Member's Bill, the debate included contributions from the Foreign Secretary William Hague and the Shadow Foreign Secretary Douglas Alexander. The debates analysed are the second and third readings of the Bill;
- Nigel Farage's party conference speech from 20 September 2013. As the leader of the hard eurosceptic United Kingdom Independence Party (UKIP), Farage holds an important position in the British discourse on Europe (Todd 2015). His party conference speech sets out the UKIP position and foretells the tone of his later contributions in the referendum campaign;
- Newspaper editorials from *The Times, Daily Mail, Daily Mirror* and *The Sun*.

In what follows, we first characterize the main points and voices in the 2013 discourse, and then re-examine the particular texts and phrases for instances of proximization.

From Sovereignty to Immigration

The immigration and anti-migration themes in UK's 2013 discourse are never addressed in isolation from the general theme of Britain's sovereignty and democracy. This theme is dominated by those who proclaim dissatisfaction with what they see as negative consequences of EU membership for UK's political and socio-economic freedoms. David Cameron is an important voice here, addressing issues of sovereignty and democracy in detail during his Bloomberg speech. He makes an explicit link between identity and foreign policy as follows:

(1) I know that the United Kingdom is sometimes seen as an argumentative and rather strong-minded member of the family of European nations. And it's true that our geography has shaped our psychology. We have the character of an island nation – independent, forthright, passionate in defence of our sovereignty. We can no more change this British sensibility than we can drain the English Channel. And because of this sensibility, we come to the European Union with a frame of mind that is more practical than emotional. For us, the European Union is a means to an end – prosperity, stability, the anchor of freedom and democracy both within Europe and beyond her shores – not an end in itself. (Cameron 2013)

Cameron goes on to note that 'there is a gap between the EU and its citizens which has grown dramatically in recent years. And which represents a lack of democratic accountability and consent that is felt particularly acutely in Britain'. He similarly affirms that 'there is a growing frustration that the EU is seen as something that is done to people rather than acting on their behalf' and that 'democratic consent for the EU in Britain is now wafer thin'. This leads him to conclude that 'we need to have a bigger and more significant role for national parliaments. There is not, in my view, a single European demos. It is national parliaments, which are, and will remain, the true source of real democratic legitimacy and accountability in the EU' (Cameron 2013). These excerpts show Cameron advocating British exceptionalism and enacting political distinction by reference to an 'independent' and 'forthright' country that is an 'island nation'. This reference to an 'island nation' is a form of intertextuality, in that it is a programmatic deictic catchphrase, bringing to mind Churchillian wartime speeches. Cameron rejects the notion of a 'single European demos' (a single 'European self') and prioritizes national parliaments, thereby privileging the 'national self' and rejecting a shared sense of European identity. Doing so, he apparently confirms Marcussen et al.'s (1999, p. 628) observation that 'classical Anglo-Saxon notions of political order emphasize parliamentary democracy and external sovereignty' and that 'there is not much room for "Europe" or "Europeanness" in British political space'. This naturally implies that any act performed in the interest of 'Europe' is potentially anti-British and can be considered a threat (Todd 2015).

Conservative backbenchers take these arguments further still, often arguing for a defense of British sovereignty through reference to history and especially the World War II. Richard Shepherd (C(onservative)) asserts:

(2) This vote, what we decide and what people in the future decide will determine the character and strength of our national constitutional history, which is being threatened. Why should we defer in such an adventure, when this is the most remarkable and ancient of all the democratic communities within western Europe? Why? (Hansard 2013–2014, p. 1201)

William Cash (C) makes an intertextual reference to Churchill, stating: 'People have fought and died. The only reason we live in the United Kingdom in peace and prosperity is because, in the second and first world wars, we stood up for that freedom and democracy. Churchill galvanised the British people to stand up for the very principles that are now at stake' (Hansard 2013–2014, p. 1210). Finally, Gordon Henderson (C) argues:

(3) It is inconceivable that only 30 years after the end of the second world war, the British people would have willingly embarked on a programme to hand over swathes of their hard-won sovereignty to another state, and let us be clear: that is what the European Union aspires to be. (Hansard 2013–2014, p. 1232)

The references to World War II and Churchill serve to consolidate the national self. They stress the centrality of the moment and prescribe the future course of action. The historical flashbacks activate reasoning by analogy: what makes current policies legitimate is, above all, their consistency with the long accepted principles and solutions. The past is thus proximized as a lesson to heed in the uncertain future. As Daddow (2006, p. 320) notes:

> This is the kind of commonsense history everyone knows even if they are not historians . . . the kind that tells us all we need to know about Europe from Britain's martial past; its encounters with the Spanish Armada, at the battle of Trafalgar, with Napoleon at Waterloo, after the let-down of Munich in 1938 and against Hitler's Germany during the Second World War.

In sum, Great Britain is linked to democratic ideals through being described as 'the most ancient and remarkable of democratic communities'. The continental Europe is in turn framed as a threat to the '[British] national constitutional history' and to the principles of freedom and democracy for which 'Churchill galvanised the British people to stand up'. This conceptual arrangement provides a solid ideological groundwork for all policy issues, including immigration.

Interestingly, Nigel Farage uses notably similar imagery and identity-based arguments to the Prime Minister Cameron and the Conservatives in building his hard-Eurosceptic case. Like Cameron, Farage claims that the UK is different because of its geography:

> (4) The fact is we just don't belong in the European Union. Britain is different. Our geography puts us apart. Our history puts us apart. Our institutions produced by that history put us apart. We think differently. We behave differently. . . . The roots go back seven, eight, nine hundred years with the Common Law. Civil rights. Habeas corpus. The presumption of innocence. The right to a trial by jury. On the continent confession is the mother of all evidence. (Farage 2013)

Farage's words are a clear example of deictic 'othering', and cementing the IDC-ODC distinction based on historical and ideological differences. Farage appeals to the weight of 'seven, eight, nine hundred years' of history, in which 'Britain is different [from continental Europe]'. He uses ethical dimensions of identity to differentiate between a British tradition of presumption of innocence and jury trial from a continental system based on confession. In the same speech Farage also affirms that 'We know that only by leaving the Union can we regain control of our borders, our parliament, democracy and our ability to trade freely with the fastest-growing economies in the world'. Implying lack of control of the '[UK] borders', he sets up a link to the immigration theme, framing it as an issue of extreme urgency and consequentiality. Like Cameron, he employs identity and cultural differentiation (Todd 2015) to serve his political cause of increasing UKIP's electoral strength and achieving a British exit from the EU.

These concerns about British sovereignty and democracy are echoed by both *The Times* and the *Daily Mail*. An editorial from *The Times* argues that 'a union worth preserving would be one that valued national sovereignty, not only for this nation but for any that wished it, and which was willing to reform to advance the prosperity of its members'. (*The Times*, 24 January 2013). The *Daily Mail* is more strongly critical:

(5) According to José Manuel Barroso, any country that wishes to re-claim powers from Brussels risks taking Europe back to the 'divisions' that led to the First World War. Doubtless, the president of the EU Commission is worried that, if the voters of Britain are given a say over our future membership by David Cameron, the verdict may not be to his liking. So, with typical contempt for democracy, he raises the spectre of the 'trenches' to try to intimidate us back into line. Yet it is Mr. Barroso's claim that the EU has brought 'peace' to Europe that is most risible. For the painful reality is that, by imposing the hopelessly-flawed single currency on its citizens, the EU has sparked terrifying social and economic unrest across great swathes of the continent. (*Daily Mail*, 13 September 2013)

The *Daily Mail* editorial includes a classic Eurosceptic trope: reference to a major European figure (Barroso), delegitimization of his or her personal position and, consequently, delegitimization of the general position of the entire adversarial party. The argument involves, again, a social element ('EU has sparked terrifying social and economic unrest across great swathes of the continent'), which paves the way for discussion of social policy issues, especially immigration. Immigration and anti-migration are thus natural follow-ups in the debate over vital national issues such as sovereignty and democracy, and their discussion tends to inherit all the major concerns and fears surrounding the national themes.

As rightly noted by Todd (2015), fears about immigration feature more heavily in newspaper editorials than in the Parliamentary discourse, though a number of backbenchers mention it. Those who do bring up the issue in connection with the debate on Europe generally do so from a negative perspective. *The Times*, the *Daily Mail* and *The Sun* all devote a considerable number of editorial column inches to problematizing immigration, while in his party conference speech Nigel Farage describes immigration as 'the biggest single issue facing the [UK]' (Farage 2013).

In the Parliamentary debate, Andrew Percy (C) makes reference to the impact of 'uncontrolled flow of EU immigration' (Hansard 2013–2014, p. 1177), while Priti Patel (C) argues that immigration rules 'have been imposed on [Britain]. We have not had a say' (p. 1236). Adam Afriyie (C) combines these two perspectives, asking 'How many times do we hear complaints about untrammelled immigration from EU countries as we no longer have the power effectively to control our own borders?' (p. 1215). He goes on to assert that 'people want to know that their Government are already fighting to get control of the [UK] borders' (p. 1238). These concerns are not limited to those on the right of the political spectrum. For example, Ian Davidson (L(abour)) states:

(6) We have to have control over our borders, which means saying to our European colleagues that we do not accept unfettered free movement of people if it is not in the United Kingdom's interest at any particular given time. (Hansard 2013–2014: 1205)

The theme of the 'loss of control' is consistent through the immigration references in the 2013 Parliamentary debate, provoking the British media to develop it further. *The Times*, although the least negative of the three right-leaning newspapers when it comes to immigration, acknowledges the calibre of the problem, connecting it to other immigration-related issues:

(7) As the country prepares for a fresh influx of migrant workers from Romania and Bulgaria, their impact may or not may not become a serious social challenge....In a new Times poll of attitudes on Europe and immigration, anxieties that Britain lacks control over its borders are the overwhelming concern of voters asked what Mr. Cameron should focus on when renegotiating the European relationship....Our poll shows that voters of all political persuasions are far more concerned about the impact of new immigration on housing and public services than on crime, inter-ethnic relations or even the availability of jobs. (*The Times*, 23 November 2013)

This excerpt illustrates another theme of the immigration discourse: 'welfare chauvinism'. The term 'welfare chauvinism' was coined by Anderson and Bjørklund (1990) to describe the perspective that state support should be restricted to national citizens and not provided to 'others'. While *The Times* represents, altogether, a moderate expression of welfare chauvinism, the stance of the other papers is more direct:

> (8) Ministers continue to duck questions about the scale of a new wave of immigration from Eastern Europe. So Migration Watch, a respected independent campaign group, has worked it out for them. The organisation estimates that up to 350,000 from Bulgaria, the EU's poorest country, and Romania will arrive over the next five years. Under EU rules, we are powerless to deny them entry or benefits once restrictions are lifted next January. (*The Sun*, 17 January 2013)

A *Daily Mail* editorial similarly complains of 'yet another sovereignty-sapping power grab' from an 'EU elite' which is 'trying to seize control not only of Britain's borders, but also the welfare state' (*Daily Mail*, 7 November 2013). Both *Daily Mail* and *The Sun* address mainly the spatial dimension of identity, raising the prospect of great numbers of impoverished migrants arriving from Balkan countries over the following years. These arrivals are linked to a set of EU rules that prevent the UK from denying the migrants either entry or benefits. In another November editorial, the *Daily Mail* goes on to picture immigration in terms of a direct threat to national identity:

> (9) For well over a decade, opinion polls have shown substantial majorities in favour of cutting immigration to a rate at which it can be comfortably absorbed. Yet in this supposed democracy, politicians have simply ignored those who elected them. Indeed, less than eight weeks from today, under orders from the EU, the Coalition plans to throw open our borders to any of 29 million Bulgarians and Romanians who choose to settle here. With our national identity at stake, the time to start listening is now. The first step must surely be to defy Brussels and declare that the UK is full up. (*Daily Mail*, 22 November 2013)

The *Daily Mail* and *The Sun* editorials bring together the main themes of British immigration discourse, construing fear via reference to loss of control and powerlessness against *waves of immigration* from the Continent. They are thus a great example of perhaps the most common metaphor running through British immigration discourse: one which recruits the CONTAINER schema to conceptualize the country (Charteris-Black 2006; Hart 2010). Charteris-Black (2006) presents evidence that metaphors construing UK as a container are a conventional feature of the discourse on immigration, reflecting and reinforcing an underlying cognitive arrangement.

The importance of the CONTAINER metaphor in political discourse and British immigration discourse in particular warrants a quick theoretical trip to understand where rhetorical powers of the metaphor reside and how they get activated. Conceptually, argues Hart (2010, 2014), the CONTAINER schema emerges from ubiquitous and reoccurring experiences with the state of containment:

> Our encounter with containment and boundedness is one of the most pervasive features of our bodily experience. We are intimately aware of our bodies as three-dimensional containers into which we put certain things (food, water, air) and out of which other things emerge (food and water wastes, air, blood, etc.). From the beginning, we experience constant physical containment in our surroundings (those things that envelop us). We move in and out of rooms, clothes, vehicles, and numerous kinds of bounded spaces. We manipulate objects, placing them in containers (cups, boxes, cans, bags, etc.). In each of these cases there are repeatable spatial and temporal organisations. In other words, there are typical schemata for physical containment. (Hart 2010, p. 160)

The CONTAINER schema consists of three structural elements: an interior and an exterior defined by a boundary. The interior also includes a CENTRE-PERIPHERY structure, and the container has, in addition, volume, which is to say a FULL-EMPTY structure (Charteris-Black 2006; Hart 2010, 2014). This cognitive arrangement holds important implications for political discourse. First, it follows from the nature of the CONTAINER schema that something is either *in* or *out* of the container; and second, the experience of containment typically involves protection from, or resistance to, external forces. As noted by Hart (2010, 2014), the conventional character of metaphors based on the CONTAINER schema increases credibility and pragmatic appeal of discourses and texts where they occur.

In the *Daily Mail* and *The Sun* editorials, the CONTAINER metaphor involves lexical items and phrases such as 'wave [of immigration]', 'absorbed', 'throw open', 'borders' and 'full up'. These items and phrases construe a scenario that justifies a restrictive immigration policy. The scenario comprises a structured set of inferences, such as the following:

- the country has a limited capacity;
- continued immigration could cause the country (the 'container') to 'rupture';
- immigration will continue as, 'under orders from the EU', the government are 'throwing open' the country's 'borders';
- the country is thus under a real and growing threat;
- the only way to offset the threat is to force the government to ignore the 'orders' and maintain a tough immigration policy.

These inferences are prompted, let us repeat, by the conventionality of the CONTAINER metaphor, which strongly facilitates reception of the conveyed insight. There are also other reception facilitators, emerging, once again, from the conceptual characteristics of the CONTAINER schema. As noted by Chilton (2004), the CONTAINER schema entails exclusivity such that members have to be in or out and that it entails protection by means of exclusion, as opposed to any other means available to human societies. This makes people accept and adapt to the reality pictured in the CONTAINER metaphor on account of their territorial instinct and in-group allegiance. Since, under the CONTAINER schema, the entity construed as 'container' is presupposed to cover a given territory and those inside the container are presupposed to own the territory it covers, the CONTAINER metaphor reinforces the general aura of stability and permanence associated with that entity. This is yet another reason why metaphors conceptualizing countries in terms of bounded entities are extremely frequent in political discourse and immigration discourse in particular. While the *Daily Mail* and *The Sun* editorials provide typical examples, the metaphors surface widely in other British papers as well:

(10) Britain is facing a nightly tidal wave of asylum seekers from Cherbourg, France's second biggest port. (*Sunday Telegraph*, 25 August 2013)
(11) Illegal entrants are at the gates but Gibraltar is standing firm. (*Sunday Times*, 8 December 2013)
(12) Britain is full to bursting point. The Government's own figures show that the UK has the highest levels of immigration in its history: in the last ten years, over two millions were added to the UK population, and the expansion shows no signs of slowing. (*The Observer*, 8 December 2013)

Finally, the 2013 immigration debate includes examples of discourse where threat, fear and public anxiety are neither metaphorized nor otherwise mitigated; they are made fully explicit:

> (13) Today *The Sun* reveals the shocking figure that nearly one in five of all rape or murder suspects is foreign. The sheer scale of crimes committed by foreigners is astonishing. Confront politicians with an embarrassing statistic and they try to get off the hook by talking about 'context'. So here's some context for that crime figure. A report published today shows that, because of a loophole in the immigration rules, more than 20,000 foreigners from outside the EU come to live here every year. It doesn't take a genius to work out that the two figures might be connected. The more foreigners who live here, the more likely it is that crimes will be committed by foreigners. The Government is trying to get a grip on immigration. The numbers overall are down. But crime figures like this show just how vital it is that loopholes are closed and sanity is restored to immigration. (*The Sun*, 6 January 2013)

PROXIMIZATION

The examples (1)–(13), comprising governmental, parliamentary and media voices and opinions, as well as a telling voice from the UKIP leader Nigel Farage, give a fair picture of the 2013 'proto-referendum' discourse in the UK. Overall, this discourse can be characterized as conceptually bipolar, recognizing the Self–Other distinction, and enacting this distinction with regard to ideological and policy issues. It seems that the presence of conceptual dichotomies in the 2013 discourse is a stable feature of the debate, unaffected by any twists or heated exchanges. Both radical voices (such as Farage's or *The Sun*'s) and more moderate positions (such as Cameron's or Shepherd's) presuppose the distinctiveness of the British state, though in different argumentation patterns. The moderate voices use it to construe an essentially ideological appeal to remain consistent with historical legacy, which emphasizes Britain's sovereignty and political autonomy. This can be seen from the argument in Cameron's speech in (1). On the other hand, radical Eurosceptics use it in a more instrumental manner, to present immigration as well as other forms of external influence (including EU policies), as a tangible threat to the daily functioning of the country.

The stability and permanence of the in/out distinction in the UK discourse constitutes the main deictic prerequisite for strategies of proximization to occur. The examples (1)–(13) contain a broad range of lexical markers of inside-deictic-centre (IDC) entities, such as 'Britain', 'British people', 'our citizens' and, finally, 'we' – the most direct marker of inclusion and in-group consolidation. At the same time, they contain lexical markers of outside-deictic-centre (ODC) entities, both those immediately encroaching on the IDC territory (immigrants) and those externally and internally responsible for influx of immigrants (EU, plus liberal and/or EU-friendly political groups and politicians within the UK). The lexical items and phrases marking these two ODC groups are, for example, 'EU Commission', 'Jose Manuel Barroso', 'our European colleagues', 'Brussels', as well as '[British] politicians ignoring [opinion of] those who elected them'. As can be seen from the last phrase, the latter group can be considered a 'home ODC' sub-group. It is related to the IDC group, and some of the member entities (such as 'ministers' in the UK government) can belong to either camp depending on who construes a given discourse. While David Cameron's speech in (1) positions the British government and its members clearly in the IDC group, *The Sun*'s editorial in (8) ('Ministers continue to duck questions about the scale of a new wave of immigration from Eastern Europe') places UK's cabinet on a par with ruling European bodies.

The main and defining element of proximization, the symbolic move-ment, can be observed in most of the examples (1)–(13). There are however two kinds of this movement, or shift, representing respectively axiological and spatial proximization. Whichever strategy is used depends, again, on the moment of the debate, type of argument, and political predispositions of the speaker. Axiological proximization serves to con-strue past behaviours, actions and events as memorable lessons for the future. It sets up a dynamic, temporal-ideological connection between the past, the present and the future, stressing the centrality of the present as the timeframe in which the future is decided. The ideological element is used to construe consistency of the present postures and actions with the long-established beliefs and values. Axiological proximization is thus, as in Shepherd's (2), Henderson's (3) or Farage's (4) discourses, an instrument to claim the rationality of the current Eurosceptic posture on account of the British heritage and the moral principles it contains and prescribes. Lexically, axiological proximization involves emphasizing the uniqueness of the British constitutional history (viz. [2]: 'the most remarkable and ancient of all the democratic communities'), defining the meaning of historical legacy for the future functioning of the country (viz. [1]:

'because of this [character, sensibility], we come to the European Union with a frame of mind that is more practical than emotional (...)', and finally, outlining current threats to that legacy and thus to the country's future (viz. [3]: 'a programme to hand over swathes of [British] hard-won sovereignty to another state').

In comparison, the reality of spatial proximization is not the past nor the future, but rather the 'here and now', which is geographically and geopolitically threatening and thus needs an immediate response in terms of specific policy or policies. As a legitimization device, spatial proximization draws on fear-generating events and images and, in contrast to axiological proximization, rarely involves an elaborate argument. The examples (1)–(13) demonstrate that instances of spatial proximization occur in discourses which address the alleged consequences of EU policies (such as the increase in British immigration rate), rather than their underlying causes (which are addressed in ideologically loaded discourses involving axiological proximization). They show that in the 2013 public debate in Britain, spatial proximization is an essentially coercive strategy, appealing to fear and general anxiety about the basic social issues, such as personal safety and economic security. Technically, the prime lexico-grammatical carriers of spatial proximization are metaphoric phrases conceptualizing the country as a CONTAINER of limited capacity and thus physically threatened by an external impact. Conceptual metaphors are particularly pervasive in media discourse, such as newspaper editorials (viz. examples [8]–[12]), which employ appealing, hard-hitting phrases ('nightly tidal wave', '[getting] full to bursting point') to construe the 'invasion'.

NOTE

1. Private Members' Bills are presented by individual MPs or members of the House of Lords ('Private Members'). They must go through the same procedures as Government bills in order to become law, but much less time is made available for them in the Parliamentary calendar. Most of them fail because there is not enough time for them to progress, rather than because of active opposition.

CHAPTER 7

Conclusion

Abstract This chapter briefly summarizes the main findings of the book and outlines analytical prospects. It reflects on the growing popularity and effectiveness of threat-based rhetoric in legitimization discourse. It provides a positive assessment of Proximization Theory as a critical-linguistic tool of analysis of threat-based discourse in various thematic domains.

Keywords Legitimization discourse · Threat-based rhetoric · Proximization Theory

This book has confirmed a deeply strategic character of public communication. As has been postulated in the opening chapter, public discourse subsumes systematic ways in which interests of the top actors, such as politicians, institutional and organizational leaders, lawmakers, and the media, are enacted linguistically. Public leaders use recurrent rhetorical patterns to exercise their power in the service of a social consensus, which entails legitimization of proposed policies and inclusion of the audience in actions prescribed by these policies. The present book has demonstrated that policy legitimization is characterized by the discursive construction of fear, which involves recognition of a gathering external threat and mobilization of the home group to approve the use of preventive measures. Threat and fear are thus core elements of public communication.

© The Author(s) 2017
P. Cap, *The Language of Fear*, DOI 10.1057/978-1-137-59731-1_7

In the book we have identified the most important strategies of threat construction and fear generation in different discourse domains, such as health, environment, cyber-technology and social migration. The analysis has revealed that a vast majority of these strategies are common to all the four discourses, allowing a conclusion that they may occur in still other domains. The most typical strategy involves setting up a dichotomous representation of the geopolitical space, marking a territorial as well as ideological opposition between the two symbolically construed camps: the 'good Self' and the 'bad Other'. The cornerstone element of this strategy is the construal of movement of the 'Other' to invade the space of the 'Self'. This construal has been identified in all the discourses analysed, notwithstanding their thematic features. It seems that the discursive construction of an ominous 'external' impact is an effective instrument of coercion across seemingly different domains, from preventive medicine, to management of climate change, to social migration and immigration.

The findings of the book have been produced within the framework of Proximization Theory (PT). The discourses analysed in the case study chapters (Chaps. 3–6) have been a new territory for PT, whose original focus was state political discourse, and the discourse of state intervention in particular. It appears that PT has been generally successful in accounting for the extended spectrum of discourses, and that its explanatory power has not been fully exploited yet. The major challenge for the future applications is, it seems, a finer, more precise account of the source, or rather sources, of the external impact. The analysis of the four discourses in the book has revealed considerable conceptual differences with regard to the status of entities perceived as 'foreign' and 'adversarial'. While the discourse of immigration tends to trace the source of the 'impact' and its reasons outside the Self camp and in the Other camp, the discourse of climate change finds many of the reasons in the ideological posture of the Self camp. This picture is even fuzzier in cyber-terrorist discourse, which frequently erases geopolitical as well as geographical distinctions and affiliations. Altogether, while PT seems to have done mostly a good job describing coercion and legitimization patterns in the discourses explored in the book, some features of these discourses have contributed new and exciting data for future upgrades of the theory.

BIBLIOGRAPHY

Adams, J. & F. Guterl. (2003, 3 November). Bringing down the Internet. *Newsweek*. http://msnbc.msn.com/id/3339638/.

Air Resources Board. (2013). *Assembly bill 32: Global warming solutions act*. California Environmental Protection Agency.

Air Resources Board. (2014). *California greenhouse gas emission inventory: 2000–2012*. California Environmental Protection Agency.

Anderson, J.G. & T. Bjørklund. (1990). Structural changes and new cleavages: the progress parties in Denmark and Norway. *Acta Sociologica, 33*, 195–217.

Axelrod, R. (1984). *The evolution of cooperation*. New York: Basic Books.

Bacevich, A. (2010). *Washington rules: America's path to permanent war*. New York: Metropolitan Books.

Bandura, A. (1986). *Social foundations of thought and action: A social cognitive theory*. Englewood Cliffs, NJ: Prentice Hall.

Bednarek, M. (2006). *Evaluation in media discourse: Analysis of a newspaper corpus*. London: Continuum.

Bendrath, R. (2003). The American cyber-angst and the real world: Any link? In R. Latham (Ed.), *Bombs and bandwidth: The emerging relationship between information technology and security* (pp. 34–51). New York: New Press.

Berglez, P. & U. Olausson. (2010). The "climate threat" as ideology: interrelations between citizen and media discourses. *Paper presented at the conference Communicating Climate Change II – Global Goes Regional*, University of Hamburg.

Bevitori, C. (2014). Values, assumptions and beliefs in British newspaper editorial coverage of climate change. In C. Hart & P. Cap (Eds.), *Contemporary critical discourse studies* (pp. 603–625). London: Bloomsbury.

© The Author(s) 2017

P. Cap, *The Language of Fear*, DOI 10.1057/978-1-137-59731-1

Boykoff, M. (2008). The cultural politics of climate change discourse in UK tabloids. *Political Geography*, *27*, 549–569.

Brown, P. & S.C. Levinson. (1987). *Politeness: Some universals in language*. Cambridge: Cambridge University Press.

Bybee, J. & S. Fleischman. (1995). *Modality in grammar and discourse*. Amsterdam: John Benjamins.

Cameron, D. (2013). David Cameron's speech on the EU. *The New Statesman*. http://www.newstatesman.com/politics/2013/01/davidcameronsspeech-eu-full-text.

Cap, P. (2002). *Explorations in political discourse. Methodological and critical perspectives*. Frankfurt am Main: Peter Lang.

Cap, P. (2006). *Legitimization in political discourse: A cross-disciplinary perspective on the modern US war rhetoric*. Newcastle: Cambridge Scholars Press.

Cap, P. (2008). Towards the proximization model of the analysis of legitimization in political discourse. *Journal of Pragmatics*, *40*, 17–41.

Cap, P. (2010). Axiological aspects of proximization. *Journal of Pragmatics*, *42*, 392–407.

Cap, P. (2013). *Proximization: The pragmatics of symbolic distance crossing*. Amsterdam: John Benjamins.

Centre for Strategic and International Studies (CSIS). (2014). *Cybercrime, cyberterrorism, cyberwarfare: Averting an electronic waterloo*. Washington, DC: CSIS Press.

Charteris-Black, J. (2006). Britain as a container: immigration metaphors in the 2005 election campaign. *Discourse & Society*, *17*, 563–582.

Chilton, P. (2004). *Analysing political discourse: Theory and practice*. London: Routledge.

Chilton, P. (2014). *Language, space and mind: The conceptual geometry of linguistic meaning*. Cambridge: Cambridge University Press.

Chovanec, J. (2010). Legitimation through differentiation: Discursive construction of Jacques *Le Worm* Chirac as an opponent to military action. In U. Okulska & P. Cap (Eds.), *Perspectives in politics and discourse* (pp. 61–82). Amsterdam: John Benjamins.

Cienki, A., B. Kaal & I. Maks. (2010). Mapping world view in political texts using Discourse Space Theory: metaphor as an analytical tool. *Paper presented at RaAM 8 conference*, Vrije Universiteit Amsterdam.

Cohn, C. (1987). Sex and death in the rational world of defense intellectuals. *Signs: Journal of Women in Culture and Society*, *12*, 13–26.

Collin, B. (2001). The future of cyberterrorism. *Proceedings of 11th Annual International Symposium on Criminal Justice Issues*, University of Illinois at Chicago.

Cosmides, L. (1989). The logic of social exchange: has natural selection shaped how humans reason? Studies within the Wason Selection Task. *Cognition*, *31*, 187–276.

Daddow, O.J. (2006). Euroscepticism and the culture of the discipline of history. *Review of International Studies*, *32*, 309–328.

Daily Mail. (2013a, 13 September). EU must be joking! *Daily Mail.*

Daily Mail. (2013b, 7 November). We don't have room for another London. *Daily Mail.*

Daily Mail. (2013c, 22 November). Brussels and why Mr Cameron can no longer ignore the people on immigration. *Daily Mail.*

Dunmire, P. (2011). *Projecting the future through political discourse: The case of the bush doctrine.* Amsterdam: John Benjamins.

Eriksson, J. (2001). Cyberplagues, IT, and security: threat politics in the information age. *Journal of Contingencies and Crisis Management*, *9*, 210–222.

Fairclough, N. (1989). *Language and power.* London: Longman.

Farage, N. (2013). Nigel Farage's speech at the UKIP conference. *The Spectator.* http://blogs.spectator.co.uk/coffeehouse/2013/09/nigelfaragessspeech-full-text-and-audio/.

Fauconnier, G. (1985). *Mental spaces: Aspects of meaning construction in natural language.* Cambridge: Cambridge University Press.

Fauconnier, G. & M. Turner. (2002). *The way we think: Conceptual blending and the mind's hidden complexities.* New York: Basic Books.

Festinger, L. (1957). *A theory of cognitive dissonance.* Stanford, CA: Stanford University Press.

Fetzer, A. & G. Lauerbach (Eds.). (2007). *Political discourse in the media.* Amsterdam: John Benjamins.

Gavins, J. (2007). *Text world theory: An introduction.* Edinburgh: Edinburgh University Press.

Gellman, B. (2012, 27 June). Cyber-attacks by Al Qaeda feared. *Washington Post.* http://www.washingtonpost.com/ac2/wp-dyn/A50765-2002Jun26.

Gough, V. & M. Talbot. (1996). "Guilt over games boys play": Coherence as a focus for examining the constitution of heterosexual subjectivity on a problem page. In C.R. Caldas-Coulthard & M. Coulthard (Eds.), *Texts and practices: Readings in critical discourse analysis* (pp. 214–230). London: Routledge.

Graham, S. (2004). War in the "weirdly pervious world": infrastructure, demodernisation, and geopolitics. *Paper presented at the conference on Urban Vulnerability and Network Failure*, University of Salford.

Grice, P. (1975). Logic and conversation. In P. Cole & J.L. Morgan (Eds.), *Syntax and semantics 3: Speech acts* (pp. 41–58). New York: Academic Press.

Groom, N. (2000). Attribution and averral revisited: Three perspectives on manifest intertextuality in academic writing. In P. Thompson (Ed.), *Patterns and perspectives: Insights into EAP writing practices* (pp. 15–27). Reading: CALS.

Habermas, J. (1981). *Theorie des kommunikativen Handelns.* Frankfurt am Main: Suhrkamp.

Hansard. (2013–2014). *House of Commons Debates*, vol. 565–571.

Hart, C. (2010). *Critical discourse analysis and cognitive science: New perspectives on immigration Discourse.* Basingstoke: Palgrave Macmillan.

Hart, C. (2014). *Discourse, grammar and ideology. Functional and cognitive perspectives.* London: Bloomsbury.

Hart, C. & P. Cap (Eds.). (2014). *Contemporary critical discourse studies.* London: Bloomsbury.

Hartman, R. (2002). *The knowledge of good: Critique of axiological reason.* Amsterdam: Rodopi.

Hockett, C. (1960). The origin of speech. *Scientific American, 203,* 88–96.

Horn, L. (2004). Implicature. In L. Horn & G. Ward (Eds.), *The handbook of pragmatics* (pp. 3–28). Oxford: Blackwell.

Hunston, S. (2000). Evaluation as the planes of discourse: Status and value in persuasive texts. In S. Hunston & G. Thompson (Eds.), *Evaluation in text: Authorial stance and the construction of discourse* (pp. 176–207). Oxford: Oxford University Press.

Huntington, S. (2004). *Who are we: The challenges to America's national identity.* New York: Simon & Schuster.

Jarvis, L. (2016). Unpacking cyberterrorism discourse: Specificity, status and scale in news media constructions of threat. *European Journal of International Security, 16,* 20–35.

Jary, M. (2010). *Assertion.* Basingstoke: Palgrave Macmillan.

Jowett, G.S. & V. O'Donnell. (1992). *Propaganda and persuasion.* Newbury Park, CA: Sage.

Kiesler, C., B. Collins & N. Miller. (1969). *Attitude change: A critical analysis of theoretical approaches.* New York: Wiley.

Krzyżanowski, M. (2009). Europe in crisis: discourses on crisis-events in the European press 1956–2006. *Journalism Studies, 10,* 18–35.

Lakoff, G. & M. Johnson. (1980). *Metaphors we live by.* Chicago: University of Chicago Press.

Levelt, W.J. (1989). *Speaking: From intention to articulation.* Cambridge, MA: The MIT Press.

Levinson, S.C. (1983). *Pragmatics.* Cambridge: Cambridge University Press.

Levinson, S.C. (2000). *Presumptive meanings: The theory of generalized conversational implicature.* Cambridge, MA: The MIT Press.

Levinson, S.C. (2003). *Space in language and cognition: Explorations in cognitive diversity.* Cambridge: Cambridge University Press.

Mann, W. & S. Thompson. (1988). Rhetorical Structure Theory: a theory of text organization. *Text, 8,* 243–281.

Marcussen, M., T. Risse, D. Engelmann-Martin, H. Knopf & K. Roscher. (1999). Constructing Europe? The evolution of French, British and German nation state identities. *Journal of European Public Policy, 6,* 614–633.

Martin, J.R. & R. Wodak (Eds.). (2003). *Re/reading the past. Critical and functional perspectives on time and value.* Amsterdam: John Benjamins.

McGray, D. (2003). The minister of net defense. *Wired* 11. http://www.wired.com/wired/archive/11.05/schmidt.html.

Porteus, L. (2001, 15 May). Feds still need to define role in tackling cyberterror, panelists say. *GovExec.com.* http://www.govexec.com/dailyfed/0501/051501td.htm.

Poulsen, K. (2003, 31 July). Official: cyberterror fears missed real threat. *SecurityFocus.com.* http://www.securityfocus.com/news/6589.

Sandwell, B. (2006). Monsters in cyberspace: cyberphobia and cultural panic in the information age. *Information, Communication & Society, 9*, 39–61.

Schwartau, W. (1994). *Information warfare: Cyberterrorism - Protecting your personal security in the electronic age.* New York: Thunder's Mouth Press.

Semino, E. (2008). *Metaphor in discourse.* Cambridge: Cambridge University Press.

Sherif, M. & C. Hovland. (1961). *Social judgment: Assimilation and contrast effects in communication and attitude change.* New Haven, CT: Yale University Press.

Silberstein, S. (2004). *War of words.* London: Routledge.

Sontag, S. (1978). *Illness as metaphor.* New York: Farrar, Straus and Giroux.

Specter, M. (2001, 28 May). The doomsday click: how easily could a hacker bring the world to a standstill? *The New Yorker.*

Sperber, D. (2000). Metarepresentations in an evolutionary perspective. In D.Sperber (Ed.), *Metarepresentation: A multidisciplinary perspective* (pp. 117–138). New York: Oxford University Press.

Stibbe, A. (2014). An ecolinguistic approach to Critical Discourse Studies. *Critical Discourse Studies, 11*, 117–128.

The Sun. (2013a, 6 January). Psst, Dave … hurry up! *The Sun.*

The Sun. (2013b, 17 January). Border alert. *The Sun.*

The Times. (2013a, 24 January). In or out. *The Times.*

The Times. (2013b, 23 November). Boundaries of welfare. *The Times.*

Todd, J. (2015). *The British self and continental other: A discourse analysis of the United Kingdom's relationship with Europe.* Oslo: Arena.

Van Eemeren, F. & R. Grootendorst. (2004). *A systematic theory of argumentation.* Cambridge: Cambridge University Press.

Van Leeuwen, T. & R. Wodak. (1999). Legitimizing immigration control: a discourse-historical analysis. *Discourse Studies, 10*, 83–118.

Van Rijn-van Tongeren, G. (1997). *Metaphors in medical texts.* Amsterdam: Rodopi.

Vegh, S. (2012). *Disrupting the status quo: non-traditional uses of the Internet as a political force,* Ph.D. thesis, University of Maryland.

Verton, D. (2003). *Black ice: The invisible threat of cyberterrorism.* New York: McGraw Hill.

Wallace, C. (2002, 16 September). Internet as weapon: experts fear terrorists may attack through cyberspace. *ABC News.com.* http://abcnews.go.com/sec tions/wnt/DailyNews/cyberterror020913.html.

Werth, P. (1999). *Text worlds: Representing conceptual space in discourse.* Harlow: Longman.

Wieczorek, A. (2013). *Clusivity: A new approach to association and dissociation in political discourse.* Newcastle: Cambridge Scholars Publishing.

Yould, R. (2003). Beyond the American fortress: Understanding homeland security in the information age. In R. Latham (Ed.), *Bombs and bandwidth: The emerging relationship between information technology and security* (pp. 70–98). New York: New Press.

Zimbardo, P. & M. Leippe. (1991). *The psychology of attitude change and social influence.* New York: McGraw-Hill.

INDEX

© The Author(s) 2017
P. Cap, *The Language of Fear*, DOI 10.1057/978-1-137-59731-1

CPSIA information can be obtained
at www.ICGtesting.com
Printed in the USA
LVOW13*1800191017
553036LV00015B/359/P

DATE DUE

			PRINTED IN U.S.A.